Thank You!

In many ways, numerous Jewish professionals and scholars helped with this project. I am grateful to all of them for lending their wisdom and support to this book. They gave of their time, shared their knowledge, and provided invaluable words of encouragement to me to continue and complete this project. They are listed with their position when this book was being written.

They include: Rabbi **Kassel Abelson** of the Rabbinical Assembly, **Gad Ben Ari** of the World Zionist Organization, **Marcia Bloomberg** of the Jewish Federation of Cleveland, Rabbi **Nina Cardin** from *Sh'ma Magazine* and the National Center for Jewish Healing, Rabbi **Norman J. Cohen** of Hebrew Union College (HUC), **Irving Cramer** of Mazon, Rabbi **Joseph Edelheit** of Temple Israel (Minneapolis), **David W. Epstein** of *The American Rabbi*, Rabbi **Jerome Epstein** of United Synagogue of America, **Allan Finkelstein** of the Jewish Community Center Association, Rabbi **Lori Forman** of the New York City Federation for Jewish Service, Rabbi **Herb Friedman** of the Wexner Heritage Foundation, author **Blu Greenberg**, **J.J. Greenberg** of the Jewish Life Network, Rabbi **Yitz Greenberg** of the National Jewish Center for Learning and Leadership (CLAL), **Dru Greenwood** of the UAHC-CCAR Department of Outreach, Rabbi **Irwin Groner** of the Shaarey Zedek Congregation (Detroit), Rabbi **Hayim Herring** of the Minneapolis Federation for Jewish Service, **Carolyn Hessel** of the Jewish Book Council, Dr. **Larry A. Hoffman** of HUC, **Avraham Infeld** of the Melitz Institute (Jerusalem), Rabbi **Rob Kahn** of Beth El Synagogue (Minneapolis), **Max Kleinman** of the MetroWest Federation for Jewish Service, author **Leslie Koppelman Ross**, **Lydia Kukoff** of the Jewish Community Center on the Upper West Side (New York), Rabbi **Irwin Kula** of CLAL, Rabbi **Nathan Laufer** of the Wexner Heritage Foundation, Rabbi **David Lieber** of the University of Judaism, Rabbi **Aryeh Meir** of the American Jewish Committee, Dr. **Carl Sheingold** of the Council of Jewish Federations (CJF), Rabbi **Alan Silverstein** of the Rabbinical Assembly, author and scholar Rabbi **Joseph Telushkin**, **Dr. Gary Tobin** of Brandeis University, **Jonathan Woocher** of the Jewish Educational Society of North America, and Rabbi **Gerald Zelizer** of Neve Shalom (New Jersey).

I give credit and thanks to these people for helping make this book a reality. They provided me with hundreds of suggestions for this book, and even though I did not include every suggestion, I carefully considered each and every one. Therefore, any errors or omissions in this book are, of course, my responsibility.

HOW TO
GET MORE OUT OF BEING JEWISH
EVEN IF:

A. You are not sure you believe in God,

B. You think going to synagogue is a waste of time,

C. You think keeping kosher is stupid,

D. You hated Hebrew school, or

E. All of the above!

by Gil Mann

Leo & Sons
PUBLISHING

Minneapolis, Minnesota, USA

A Friendly Copyright Notice

6th Edition

Library of Congress Cataloging-in-Publication Data
  Mann, Gil
     How to get more out of Being Jewish Even If:
     Bibliography; p.
     ISBN 0-9651709-2-6

     1. Judaism. 2. Jewish way of life. 3. Jews—Attitudes.
  4. Jews—Identity. 5. Judaism—20th Century—United States.
  6. Jews—Secularism. 7. Spiritual life—Judaism. I. Title.
  296.74M281   Library of Congress Record # 96-75728

    10   9   8   7

Printed in the United States of America by:
Leo & Sons Publishing
A Division of On Line Marketing, Inc.
175 Oregon Avenue South
Minneapolis, MN 55426
Phone: 763-545-3666
Phone: 1-800-304-9925
Fax: 763-542-0171
Email: LeoPublish@aol.com
Website: www.BeingJewish.org

Dedication

This book is dedicated with love to:

My parents Vivian and Arie Mann and Leonard and Fay Ribnick
for giving me Jewish roots and nourishment,

My wife Debbie who is always giving to me
beyond what I ask or deserve, and

My kids: Josh, Nomi, Danny and Shosh
who give me frequent happiness, an occasional sleepless night
and constant reminding of what really matters in life.

Contents

A Few Notes About This Book From the Author

I admit this is not your normal book. The unusual title alone may have tipped you off, or maybe it was the friendly copyright notice on page iv. Inside, you will quickly see that there is more that is atypical. For example, this book is both fiction and nonfiction. Plus, most of the book is written in an unconventional format: dialogue. To help you get the most out of your reading, I offer the following brief tidbits.

Who is this book for?

If you are Jewish, there is a good chance you will find something of value in this book. More specifically, this book has something for you if any of the following describe you:

- You chose any of the answers (A through E) in the title of this book,

- You care about being Jewish but have a hard time explaining why,

- You feel proud to be Jewish but are not sure how to instill that pride in your children or grandchildren,

- You feel bad or guilty in any way about your Judaism,

- You're not sure how you feel about your Judaism,

- You're active as a professional or volunteer in a Jewish organization or institution,

- You're in love with a Jewish person, or

- You're just curious about Judaism.

What will you get out of this book?

Everyone is different, of course, but at the very least, you will learn how others see and understand their Judaism. You will likely find that many of your sentiments and questions about Judaism are shared by others. This should give you comfort. If you are a professional or lay leader in a Jewish organization, you will gain some insight into what many "Jews on the street" are thinking. Finally, whether you consider yourself to be actively practicing Judaism or not, you will also likely find some answers and ideas about Judaism that are new and helpful.

How to read this book.

I suggest that you first read chapters 1 and 2. After that, you could read the chapters in any order. Most people have told me that they prefer to read only one or two chapters in a sitting to better digest the dialogue. On the other hand, others have told me they quickly read from cover to cover. I have also been amazed (and touched) by the number of people who have told me they read the book twice—once quickly and the second time slowly. One person even told me he read parts of the book out loud at his Passover seder. You have a lot of options.

What's the point of this book?

One person who read an early manuscript sent me a note that summed up the point of this book well. She wrote: "This book stimulated me to examine what being Jewish means to me in a nonthreatening way."

While I hope you have a similar reaction, I want to emphasize that this book is not intended to bring you to any specific Jewish destination. In other words, this book is not meant to convince you to adopt any specific level of Jewish practice, observance, or affiliation. Rather, it is meant to help you start or continue a search of how Judaism can add meaning to your life. This book recognizes that where you decide to go with your Judaism is a personal matter. What is important about this book—and Judaism for that matter—is the journey. Bon voyage!

Chapter 1
The Birth of This Book

When it was over, I had trouble sleeping. Beforehand, I wasn't quite sure what to expect, but I suspected it would be powerful. I was right. Six Jews, five of them complete strangers to me, had agreed to come to a focus group and share their thoughts about being Jewish. They had a lot to say.

I had received their names from friends of friends. Their names led to other names. My phone call to each of them was similar, as were their responses to me. When I made the first calls, I was worried that the topic would be too sensitive. I was tentative:

"Hi, my name is Gil Mann. I got your name from so and so and I'm not selling anything."

Pause—silence.

"What I am doing is writing a book about being Jewish that I'm hopeful you can help me with."

"About being Jewish? What do you mean?" As I feared, the response was suspicion bordering on hostility. Cautiously, I continued.

"I'm inviting five or six Jews who are not actively involved with the organized Jewish community to a focus group, and basically, I want to listen. I want to hear what you think of Judaism. I'll tell you the title of the book, that for now I'm using as a working title, which more or less sums up what I'm doing."

Pause—silence.

"It's called *How to Get Something Out of Being Jewish Even if You Think Keeping Kosher Is Stupid.*"

This almost always provoked a laugh or an audible smirk. From this point on, the tension of our conversations evaporated. The person would usually then make a comment like, "That sounds interesting. I think I'd like to come —if nothing else, to hear what other people had to say."

Six of the first seven people I called said they were interested in sharing what was on their mind. I was astonished at the response rate I was encountering. But this was just the beginning; I was even more amazed at what they had to say and at the candor and intensity with which they expressed themselves.

That first focus group happened to fall on the day after Yom Kippur. Four of the six people who came were not even aware that Yom Kippur had just occurred. I was taken aback. I expected that they might say that they did not attend High Holiday services, but not that it was "just another day in the week." To me it seemed that even most non-Jews know when Yom Kippur appears on the calendar, yet these Jews did not. In spite of this, these people had very strong feelings and opinions about Judaism and being Jewish.

One particularly powerful exchange occurred when one of the single men who came was explaining that in his entire life, he had been to a synagogue about as often as he had been to a Unitarian church—"a few times." He said that in his family he was now the third generation of nonreligious Jews and that, though he considered himself to be Jewish, he did not prefer the synagogue over the church, nor could he state what being Jewish meant to him.

He went on to explain that he did not feel strongly about marrying a Jewish or non-Jewish woman. At this point, a woman participant interrupted him. She leaned forward in her chair and said painfully to his face, "If I don't give my child any religious training, is she going to end up like you?" Her comment was remarkable to me because she was one of the people who did not realize that Yom Kippur had just passed, nor did she seem to care.

That was typical of an evening full of touching and heartfelt comments as well as forceful exchanges that usually were expressions of agreement or enhancement of a statement someone else had made. Several other times, people sharply disagreed with each other.

I had told them on the phone that the focus group would last two hours. After two and a half hours I felt I should at least try to keep my promise to them, and I brought the passionate dialogue to a close.

As I went around the room for their final comments, the room felt heavy and light at the same time. The gist of the comments was: "This is the first time in 20 years that I've spoken about some of the subjects we discussed, and I can't believe how comfortable I felt here tonight, saying these things to strangers, who somehow do not feel that strange to me simply because we're all Jewish." After their final comments, they stayed even longer, socializing with each other and asking me questions.

The night ended with a flip comment one of them made that for me was both profound and sad. They were bundling up to go out into a 40° autumn night. As the door opened and a brisk breeze came in, one of them said, "Well, off to the fringe we go." I can still feel the physical and emotional chill of that moment.

The discussion that night had hit many nerves, not the least of which were mine — which explains why I had trouble sleeping. That evening, I heard a lot of potent arguments, challenging questions, and raw emotion. This book attempts to capture some of what I heard that night and in other focus groups and interviews, and also to provide some answers.

"Affiliated" Jew: A Loaded and Misleading Term

That first focus group, of course, was just a beginning. A total of 12 focus groups were conducted with many types of Jews.* Ten of these groups were

---

*Six of the focus groups were conducted by the Jewish Life Network, Chaverim Kol Yisrael. I am indebted to them for their help with this project.

conducted before the book was written, and two were with Jewish people who read early versions of the manuscript. In addition, I formally and informally interviewed many dozens of Jews of all stripes from all over the country. Over a period of about four years, I heard over 150 Jews express their sentiments about being Jewish. I should point out that during this process, I never intended, nor do I claim today, that the Jews who I heard be considered a scientific study or sampling.

At first, I concentrated on Jews who were "unaffiliated," but from the very first focus group found that I had a problem with this often-used term. The problem: Who or what is an affiliated Jew? If you belong to a synagogue but hardly ever attend services, does that mean you're affiliated? If you do not belong to a synagogue but enroll your kids in a Jewish nursery school, does that qualify as affiliated? Are you affiliated or "un" if you contribute money to a Jewish cause or read a Jewish publication or follow events in Israel but never walk through the doors of a Jewish organization? How do you define a Jew who proudly identifies as a Jew but does not practice any form of traditional Judaism?

So, rather than try to define "affiliated," or judge the quality of anyone's Jewishness, I sought to hear from a range of Jews about how they practiced their Judaism and why.

I heard from Jews who belonged to synagogues, volunteered for Jewish causes, and considered themselves very connected to Judaism. On the other side were people like those in that first focus group, who consisted of Jews who have little or no attachment to organized Jewish life. Plus, I heard from many people who were in between. The majority of the people I heard fell within a range of Jews who practiced little or no form of traditional Judaism and did not feel attached at all to Jewish life, to Jews who belonged to a synagogue or temple but did not attend weekly services. The 1990 National Jewish Population Survey seems to suggest that most American Jews fall within this range.

Most of the Jews I heard were within this range of affiliation or practice:

LESS   MORE

Completely unattached   Belonged to synagogue/temple
to organized Jewish Life   but did not attend weekly

During my research, I wanted to hear what these Jews had to say, and conse-quently I said as little as possible. I received an earful as I gathered infor-mation for this book. I had little problem getting them to talk to me. In fact, people seemed to enjoy the opportunity. More than once I heard the senti-ment that "This is the first time I've ever been asked about what being Jewish means to me." Or, "No one has ever asked me about my Jewish background or upbringing before." I almost had more of a problem getting people to stop talking once they had begun.

There was a healthy dose of emotion in what they had to say about their Judaism. For most people, the feelings were mixed. The extent of negative emotion went from apathy to anger. I perceived that the most dominant negative emotions were sadness and confusion.

While harboring these negative feelings, most people simultaneously had positive feelings. These included pride, desire and curiosity to know more, and what I would call an almost innate inner urge to perpetuate Judaism. These conflicting emotions combined with the many things people had to say about Judaism shaped the six themes of this book.

The Themes of This Book

During the focus groups and interviews, six main themes surfaced repeatedly. Together they can be summed up in a central question: "Why be Jewish?" Most striking to me was that this question and these themes were issues for Jews regardless of their background, age, sex, marital status (including intermarrieds), or current level of Jewish connection and practice. Because of this, here I need to make a very important point: This is not a book about the "unaffiliated"—whatever that is. I heard the six themes of this book raised over and over again by all kinds of Jews. So whether you consider yourself to be "affiliated," "unaffiliated," or something else, I suspect that some or all of the themes will likely resonate for you as well.

In focus groups and interviews, some people raised all six issues and others raised only one or two of them. Everyone, however, seemed interested in an answer to their personal question: "Why should I and my children carry on Judaism?" To provide answers to that question, the rest of this book is organized in six chapters. Each chapter focuses on one of the six themes that people raised (though there is some overlap between chapters). The six themes are:

Chapter 2.
"What Is Judaism Anyway?"

Virtually every person I asked to define Judaism gave me a different definition or version of an answer. No wonder there is a "Jewish continuity crisis" in this country; many American Jews are not even sure what Judaism is. They told me all kinds of things such as: Judaism is a religion, it's a race, it's an identity, it's a culture, it's a faith, it's a people… it's confusing! This chapter should eliminate this confusion with a simple yet rich definition that you can live with easily and happily.

Chapter 3.
"I'm Not Even Sure I Believe in God"

I was amazed not only that this subject came up as a major issue but also because the topic seemed to dominate so many of the conversations and all other subjects. People repeatedly said, "If my faith is shaky, why should I and how can I be Jewish?" Many people spoke about their questions of faith with great unease. They felt embarrassed. They felt guilty. They felt they were bad Jews. They were comforted to learn that their views were very typical or "normal." There is also relief in understanding what I call the "Christianization of Judaism." If your faith is less than rock solid, stop calling yourself a bad Jew. Instead, read this chapter. It should provide you with some comfort and answers as well.

Chapter 4.
"There Is No Spirituality for Me in Synagogues and Prayer"

Ouch! This is a tough area, with complaints from here until forever. Responding to these complaints is not easy. I was left with the strong impression that Jewish organizations have a lot of work to do to remedy the issues that were raised. Still, if you have an open mind, this chapter offers some ideas that can help you find spirituality or, minimally, some personal meaning and ways to become a better person through Jewish worship — whether by yourself or with others.

Chapter 5.
"I Have a Love-Hate Relationship With the Jewish Community"

While people expressed much disapproval of the Jewish community as being cliquish and elitist, they spent just as much time talking about how they somehow felt membership — or at least they wanted to be included. Stated another way, I often heard during the same conversation: "Why can't the Jewish community stay out of my personal business?" and also "Why do I find that

I often gravitate to other Jewish people?" This chapter addresses these and other similar questions about Jewish peoplehood to give you insight into why being Jewish includes both a difficult and a wonderful attachment to the Jewish community.

Chapter 6.
"The Jewish Code of Behavior Is Out of Touch and Out of Date"

Many people told me they have a hard time relating to the behavior dictated by Jewish law and ritual. No one ever provided them with a meaningful explanation of Jewish ethics and values—the rationale behind these ancient rules and regulations. This chapter shows that these Jewish ethics and values are ingrained in many of us and influence our day-to-day thinking and behavior—regardless of whether or not we are conversant in Jewish ethics or actively practice any Jewish laws. Also in this chapter, there is a good chance you will find that what Judaism has to say about human behavior and human potential makes sense to you. So much so that you may give fresh thought to the relevance of being Jewish today.

Chapter 7.
"Hebrew School Was Worthless and Boring"

This is one of the few statements I encountered that almost all Jews seem to be able to agree on. This is ironic and sad, given Judaism's emphasis on and reverence for learning. Clearly something is amiss in the way we teach Judaism. What can be done about it? There are suggestions in this chapter. In addition, there are some ideas here that should make you feel proud to be Jewish and that should be part of Jewish education.

The Format of This Book

Each of the six chapters that follows is a dialogue with a different person. Because these chapters are dialogues, they do not necessarily end with an obvious conclusion. Instead, the final comments point in the direction of the next chapter's subject. You may wonder why I chose a dialogue format for this book. There are two reasons: first, because I wanted to capture the tone and content of what I heard as closely as possible; and second, because I wanted to make reading this book accessible and easy. The comments I heard from the many people who were kind enough to read this book when it was in manuscript form validated for me that the dialogue accomplished both goals. I hope that you too find it easy reading.

You will see that the chapters begin with a brief introduction and a profile of the person speaking in that chapter's dialogue. As you read the profiles of the six people in this book, you may think you recognize someone you know. This is not a coincidence, because the profiles are fictionized versions of real people and actual comments I heard. The people may also seem familiar because, as mentioned earlier, I found that, regardless of their backgrounds, almost every person I heard expressed similar comments. In fact, a number of times during focus groups people said, "I thought I was the only one who felt this way. It's nice to know that I'm not alone."

I promised all these people that I would not identify them. Instead, the profiles and statements in this book are composites that are typical of the many people and different personalities I encountered. I hope as you read, you often think: "Hey, I know someone just like that… in fact, that sounds like something I might say."

The Responses

Unlike the focus groups and interviews where I just listened, the dialogue in this book includes responses from me. In reality, the responses are also a composite of numerous voices. Many of the responses are based on my thoughts about Judaism. Many others are based on ideas I read or heard from rabbis and Jewish authorities. Most of these people are listed with my gratitude at the beginning of this book.

As I formulated the responses for this book, my thinking was often influenced by other people, with ideas borrowed from many sources. In particular, I must acknowledge that many responses were influenced by four knowledgeable and important modern Jewish thinkers: Rabbi Irwin Kula, Rabbi Harold Kushner, Rabbi Joseph Telushkin, and Dennis Prager. I regret that in the dialogue sections of this book, the format does not lend itself well to attributing their ideas and others on a case-by-case basis. I hope all the contributors of those ideas will forgive me. At the same time, I have merged and purged ideas and added my own, so I do not mean to imply that the responses have been endorsed officially by any one person or organization. In sum, then, even though many ideas were contributed by others, the responses should be considered a reflection of my personal conclusions about Judaism.

As you read the responses, I hope you think, "I didn't know that about Judaism. I'd be interested to find out more." If that is the case for you, the end of the book offers some suggestions of where you might look.

At the end of each chapter are a few additional responses I call "Afterthoughts." These afterthought sections are a result of comments I heard from people who read early versions of this book. Over 60 people around the country reviewed versions of this book. If I named all of these people, this section would sound like the Academy Awards. Plus, I would probably leave out someone by mistake. Instead, here I say a large "thank you." From all of these wonderful people I heard countless valuable corrections, comments, and questions. In these short afterthought sections, I have tried to respond to some of their comments that I thought others might also have. Also at the end of each chapter, I leave you with some questions relating to that chapter that you may wish to think about.

My Background

Since I am assuming responsibility for the responses, you deserve to know a bit about my background. First, I am not a rabbi. My personal level of observance — like keeping kosher — has varied greatly throughout my life and continues to go up and down. What has remained constant is that being Jewish has always been important to me. Since I was a child, I have almost instinctively been proud to be Jewish — though until recently, I couldn't clearly articulate why. Now I can, because as an adult, I have devoted much time and effort to learning about Judaism, including three years of intensive Jewish study in a program known as the Wexner Heritage Foundation.

I grew up in a non-Jewish suburb of Minneapolis. I attended public schools that were predominantly gentile. In my high school class of 700-something, there were about a dozen Jewish students. My parents' home was not kosher or particularly religious, but we all knew we were Jewish. The two main reasons were my parents. My mom was a Hebrew school teacher and my dad was an Israeli (a very secular one). All the reminding we needed that we were Jewish was hearing my mother and father speaking in Hebrew when they did not want us to understand what they were talking about — which was often.

In addition to the Hebrew spoken by my parents, as I grew up, I was exposed to a lot of Judaism. I visited Israel regularly, attended Jewish camps as both a camper and a counselor, and was a teacher for many years at my synagogue.

I should point out that just because my mom taught Hebrew did not mean I behaved better at Hebrew school than anyone else. In fact, I got into more trouble than my friends. I attended afternoon Hebrew school all the way through high school — my mom made me. Unlike my friends, when I was rowdy (a daily occurrence), after throwing me out of class, my teachers just went down the hall to complain to my mother.

The net result of this upbringing was that my attraction to Judaism was strong enough that while in college, I actually gave thought to attending rabbinical school. But I decided not to for numerous reasons — not the least of which was that I did not like services! (I didn't think they would let me go through six years of rabbinical school and skip all the services.)

Instead, I majored in political science and broadcast journalism. My career began in TV news and eventually evolved into business. In 1983, my wife and I started a company producing computer training video courses that we marketed nationally mainly to Fortune 500 companies and government. The business grew to become an industry leader with over 130 employees and offices all over the world. The success of the company has given me the opportunity to pursue this book — which is a combination of two of my interests: marketing and Judaism.

Marketing has been the aspect of business that has interested me most because I have been intrigued by customers' behavior. I like to know what they are "really" thinking and why. My experience has been that if you ask, they will frankly tell you.

In recent years, as I have sought answers to my many questions about Judaism, I have come to see that the product is quite good but sales haven't been so hot. Consequently, as part of my personal investigation of Judaism, I also became curious to know what other Jews think of Judaism. So I asked. The result of all this questioning is now in your hands.

You

In the midst of the research for this book, I was telling a friend about the powerful and abundant reaction I was receiving from the people who were speaking to me. He said, "You have obviously tapped into a source of energy that was ready to be released." If he is right, then within these pages will be something of value for you. As I mentioned, minimally, you will likely see that others share some of your views. Optimally, you will find something new and worthwhile in Judaism that can help you answer the question: **"Why be Jewish?"**

If you are currently active in the Jewish community as a lay leader or professional, this book offers you something different. You have likely heard the "continuity battle cry" that Jewish organizations can no longer continue conducting "business as usual." For any business to succeed, being mindful of customer needs and desires is critical. For you, then, I hope this book provides some guidance as you structure programs and your organization for a strong Jewish future.

An Invitation to You to Stay in Touch

Since this book was first published in 1996 a number of wonderful things have happened because of the strong positive response from readers. First of course, the book has been reprinted numerous times. But in addition to that, a series of developments have allowed readers and I to stay in touch. One of the reasons I am thrilled about this is that the comments have been so rich that a follow-up book with readers' Jewish issues, questions and comments will result.

At the end of this book are more details about all the developments since this book was first published. But up front, I want to invite you to send me your thoughts and experiences. Who knows? You may be a part of the next book — anonymously of course! You can contact me at:

Gil Mann
c/o Leo & Sons Publishing
175 Oregon Avenue South
Minneapolis, MN 55426

Fax: 763-542-0171
Email: MannGil@aol.com
Website: BeingJewish.org

I am very interested to hear from you! Thanks, happy reading, and shalom!

Chapter 2
"What Is Judaism Anyway?"

An effective way to start interviews and focus groups, I found, was simply to ask people to tell me about their Jewish upbringing. What rituals, if any, were practiced in your home? What was your parents' attitude toward Judaism? Did you have a bar/bat mitzvah? What, if any, formal Jewish education did you have? And so on.

Not only were these questions good icebreakers, the answers were interesting and often almost entertaining. I was fascinated to note that in group settings, participants gave rapt attention to each other as Jewish backgrounds and thoughts were expressed. There was often a lot of head nodding as they affirmed similar experiences and sentiments. As they told their stories, many seemed to be struggling with the question of what Judaism has to offer them in this day and age. Put another way, they just weren't sure they could find any meaning or value for their lives in Judaism.

One place where the head nodding stopped, however, was when people tried to define Judaism. This was a perplexing question to most. Very few had a crisp definition. Since this was such a challenge for most, answering questions about finding meaning and value in Judaism was all the more challenging — in some cases, not possible at all.

You will see this dynamic in this chapter. It is difficult to answer the question "Why be Jewish?" if you have a hard time first answering "What is Judaism?" Therefore, in this chapter, a definition of Judaism is offered that I hope you will find both simple and rich.

Gary

After becoming a CPA, Gary decided to also get a law degree—which he did—while working full time at a national accounting firm, all by the age of 25—which is also when he got married. Now, at 38, he is studying at night school to add an MBA to his resume. His reward for all of this hard work is a high-paying job as a top executive in a fast-growing high-tech company in Chicago.

Gary is intense and driven. Whenever he speaks, he gestures forcefully with his hands. When he listens, his eyes are focused like headlights. By his own admission, he is a type A personality, and his life reflects this intensity.

He is fit and trim, which is not surprising, since he works out or plays tennis at his health club at least four times a week. "I work hard and I play hard," he says with obvious pride. He's also very much into local sports as a spectator, provided his Bulls, Bears, or Cubs are winning. If they are losing or even playing poorly, he has no time for them.

He is clearly a forceful, confident, and successful individual. He is also a contemplative and questioning person and wonders if he has accomplished anything in his life that really matters. The one obvious exception to him is his two children… "they matter a lot." Speaking of his children seems to evoke a softer side of him. He wants to provide his children with everything, but beyond the "material goodies," as he puts it, like frequent family trips, state-of-the-art PCs, electronic gizmos, and of course, a dog, he and his wife struggle with what to give their children—especially when it comes to being Jewish.

His children are the main reason he thinks about being Jewish at all. He said he was glad to have a conversation with me because "truthfully, my life is quite full as it is. I have not felt a need to give much thought to being Jewish—until recently, that is, because of my kids. I have virtually no Jewish education, so I'm just not sure what to do for my kids. But I do have a sense that I should do something. This is hard for me, though, since my Judaism leaves me mostly frustrated and confused. I certainly don't want to pass that on to my kids."

Gary: I'm sick and tired of listening to everyone complaining about continuity and preserving Judaism. Wherever I go, I hear "we're assimilating… we're intermarrying…." I say, so what! I'm just not sure I need Judaism in my life. I'm not sure anyone needs Judaism anymore. Maybe Judaism has just outlived its usefulness. Evolution is naturally taking care of Judaism and we're becoming extinct.

Gil: *Judaism is a dinosaur?*

Gary: Maybe. I look at it this way. My brother married a gentile. She's a wonderful person and I love her like a sister. She's highly ethical and principled, she's a giving person, and… she's not Jewish. I see her and others and I'm just not sure what is so special about Judaism. Perhaps Judaism has no meaning anymore. If it did, we wouldn't be shrinking and disappearing.

Gil: *What do you mean by no meaning?*

Gary: Well, I'm not sure Judaism offers society anything that can't be found elsewhere. Personally, when I think of Judaism, spiritually it gives me next to nothing. Culturally, I feel Jewish, though I'm not sure exactly what that means. I have serious questions about all organized religions in the first place. As for Judaism, in my gut I mostly have an empty feeling — with a touch of anger — synagogues, meaningless rituals and prayer, Hebrew school, learning to "chant" for my bar mitzvah, community pressure—I could go on and on.

Gil: *Please do.*

Gary: All right. I should say up front that there is a part of this whole thing that confuses me. At best, I have muddled feelings about Judaism, and yet for some reason that I can't understand, I want my children to be Jewish—at least I think I do. I'll give you an example. My son is 10. The other day, his best friend — who is not Jewish — was over, and I overheard him ask my son if he was Jewish. And my son said, "Not really." That bothered me. But I can't come up with a good explanation of why. And since I'm not even sure "why" I want my kids to be Jewish, I'm certainly not sure what to give my kids, Jewishly speaking.

Gil: *Is there anything you received Jewishly when you were raised that you do want to give your kids?*

Gary: That is probably at the root of my confusion. I picked up a few things Jewishly that I think I'd like my kids to have. But I'm not sure. I don't think my parents gave me a lot of compelling reasons to be Jewish. Now that I'm a parent, in general, I find I either repeat or rebel from how my mom and dad parented — usually repeat, I suppose — even though I swore I never would. When it comes to Judaism, I am not exactly sure what I am repeating or why.

Gil: *So what was your Jewish upbringing like?*

Gary: I don't think my upbringing Jewishly was very unique—and parts of it I actually view favorably. My mother was much more into Judaism than my dad. My mom didn't have a lot of Jewish knowledge, but she definitely was a Jewish mama.

Gil: *Which means…*

Gary: She was into feeding us. Beyond that, she really doted on us—she still does. Even though she was not very knowledgeable and didn't go to the temple except when she had to—like High Holidays and when we were invited to a bar mitzvah—she knew that she wanted us all to go to Hebrew school and to have bar mitzvahs. So we did.

Gil: *Where was your dad on all this?*

Gary: My dad grew up in a very observant home — kosher and everything. And when he became an adult he rejected almost everything.

Gil: *Why?*

Gary: I'm not sure how strong his convictions were growing up—though he usually spoke fondly of his home and parents. As he got older, though, he began questioning a lot. I think I'm a lot like my dad in that regard. The more we questioned our Judaism, the less meaning we found. We both especially didn't like doing things by rote. My father thought Judaism was a relic from the "old country." And the Holocaust was a turning point in his losing interest in Jewish faith. He just could no longer believe in God or the idea of Jews being God's chosen people.

Gil: *So how did he act in your home?*

Gary: Basically he was indifferent about most Jewish things. Except I remember when I was a kid, he convinced my mom to switch from a Conservative synagogue to a Reform temple. As a rule, he didn't seem to care that my mom was pushing Jewish things — but he never pushed. He would just sort of go along. He did seem to be dragging his feet all the time — but he didn't complain. Like he would always "come along" with my mom and us if we went to the temple, but I could tell he didn't want to be there. Jewishly, the only thing he did seem to care about was Israel and family holiday get-togethers. Also, now that I think about it, it seems that almost all of his friends were Jewish.

> **"My father thought Judaism was a relic from the "old country." And the Holocaust was a turning point in his losing interest in Jewish faith."**

Gil: *So what are your strongest Jewish memories?*

Gary: One that comes to mind quickly is that my mom and dad were always talking about "the Jewish thing to do."

Gil: *What did they mean by that?*

Gary: They meant it positively. Like I should get an education and never stop learning. Or I remember my parents were always very concerned about any disadvantaged groups anyplace in the world. Once I asked why, and they said something like "because we're Jews. And we Jews know what it feels like to be hated or to be poor and hungry with no place to go." They always said that the Jewish thing to do is to be a "mensch." The bottom line was I think they meant act ethically. Now that I'm older, I'm not sure I agree with my parents.

Gil: *What do you mean?*

Gary: Well, I don't think being Jewish guarantees that a person will act ethically. And I think many non-Jews act ethically. Also, I don't like some of the "Jewish things to do" — like minding everyone else's business or guilting a person into making donations to charity. At the same time, I think I do know what my parents meant. I guess this is another area where I'm left searching for a good explanation for myself— and my kids.

> **"My most lasting memory of my bar mitzvah is not the event itself but being forced to go to religious school so I could have a bar mitzvah. I hated it."**

Gil: *The "Jewish thing to do" means different things to different people. I'd like to talk to you more about that, but first tell me what else do you remember?*

Gary: Like my dad, I too have fond memories of his parents, my grand-parents—they were Zayde and Bubbe. They were very religious, but they seemed so comfortable with it. Their house was always warm. And the food was great — except for the sponge cake. Boy, my grandmother made some incredible chopped liver—if that could be Judaism I'd be in heaven—and about 20 pounds heavier.

Gil: *In a way I think it is.*

Gary: Chopped liver? What?

Gil: *It's kind of a little theory of mine. I'll tell you about it in a second. But first, finish telling me about your memories. You seem to have some pretty negative feelings about the synagogue.*

Gary: You're right, though I didn't start out that way. One of my fondest memories as a little kid was going to the synagogue with my Zayde. "The Shul," my Zayde called it.

Gil: *So why are you so down on synagogue?*

Gary: Well, that was when I was a little kid. I was about six when my Zayde passed away, and then I stopped going to his shul. Since then, synagogues have felt meaningless to me — formal, almost antiseptic. This includes my parents' synagogue and their temple, and almost every other one I've visited.

Gil: *What was your bar mitzvah like?*

Gary: My most lasting memory of my bar mitzvah is not the event itself but being forced to go to religious school so I could have a bar mitzvah. I hated it. I don't remember learning anything. They tried to teach me to read and chant Hebrew. But that was hopeless. Then I had to memorize everything off of a tape. I could barely do that either. But somehow I did — sort of. My dad used to drop me off at Saturday school on his way to his work or his golf game, and I remember thinking at the time, "What's the point of this bar mitzvah? This is so stupid." The best part of my bar mitzvah, besides the presents, of course, was getting to quit Hebrew school and have a normal afternoon like all the rest of the kids. Also, my dad let me join him for golf on Saturday.

Gil: *Had I started golfing at that age... no, never mind... I would still be terrible. Anyway, that brings you to your teenage years. What Jewish memories do you have about them?*

Gary: I went one year to a Jewish summer camp, which I enjoyed. But I must say I don't remember anything that was especially Jewish about the camp, except we used a few Hebrew words and sang some Hebrew songs. I remember services were completely boring. Of course, all of the kids were Jewish, and we liked camp because we all thought we were adults—at camp it was okay and cool to get away with that adult shtick. Plus we were starting to notice the opposite sex. The whole environment was exciting and new. You know: songs, food, sounds, nature, dance, libido—not necessarily in that order.

Gil: *Now you've teased me. What about dating?*

Gary: Sorry, it's not that exciting. I tended to get involved in long, serious relationships — one of them lasted four years — but never with a Jew. In fact, I didn't date Jews. Though the crazy thing is that the first Jew I did date I married. I'll tell you something else that's weird. I often find that when I'm traveling around the country for work and I meet a Jewish person, I automatically have this unusual bond —even though I don't lead a "Jewish" life.

Gil: *Why do you think that's weird?*

Gary: Well, like I said before, for the most part, I think Judaism is meaningless today. That's why I think it's shriveling away. At the same time, for some strange reason, I find I'm often drawn toward another Jewish person in kind of an unspoken way—even though we both sort of think Judaism is meaningless. That's how I met my wife.

Gil: *For a person who finds Judaism meaningless, you seem to have fairly strong feelings.*

Gary: To be honest, when I take the time to think about Judaism, I feel confused. I just don't find good answers. But it's just not that high a priority, so I usually don't bother to think about it.

Gil: *But you obviously have thought about "your Judaism" at least occasionally. What made it a priority at those times?*

Gary: I gave the most serious thought to my being Jewish seven years ago when my father became ill and passed away. You know, I had a fair amount of contact with the rabbi, plus I was giving a lot of thought to life and death. And I guess, similarly, when I became a parent, many of the same thoughts came to mind. Both events raised a lot of issues in me.

Gil: Like what?

Gary: Well, my youngest child is starting nursery school. And she is asking me the same questions her older brother used to ask — like why does God do this and why does God do that. And I'm finding that I'm giving her the same answers I was told... even though I'm not sure I believe what's coming out of my mouth. I tell her I'm not sure—but still I have to tell her something. And my son will be 13 soon, and my wife is saying she would like him to have a bar mitzvah — even though her Jewish upbringing is similar to mine. And even though my bar mitzvah was mostly a bad experience, for some reason, I guess I also want him to have a bar mitzvah. I'm realizing that I'm making my kids Jewish and I'm not sure why.

> **"To be honest, when I take the time to think about Judaism, I feel confused. I just don't find good answers. But it's just not that high a priority..."**

Gil: Any guesses?

Gary: The best answer I can come up with is that I don't want to break the chain of Judaism. But survival for survival's sake is not good enough for me. I don't feel comfortable with that answer because I'm not sure Judaism has meaning anymore.

Gil: Tell me, how are you defining Judaism?

Gary: That's a hard question. Mostly I think Judaism is a religion. But it's also kind of a culture or race of people too, I guess.

Gil: *That's how many people describe Judaism — including many non-Jews. But it's really not very accurate.*

Gary: Wait a minute. How do you know? Are you some kind of rabbi?

Gil: *I'm not a rabbi at all. I'm a person like you who also has had many questions about Judaism. I like to think of myself as a modern person who believes in science and equality and democracy and all the other things we "sophisticated" 20th-century people believe in. My experiences with Judaism growing up have been different from yours, but still, over the years, I've had some serious doubts about whether Judaism has any meaning today.*

Gary: So why didn't you just say, "The heck with it?"

Gil: *I couldn't. Even though my parents' household was not very religious and my parents didn't keep kosher, still our house had a very strong Jewish identity.*

Gary: What do you mean?

Gil: *Well, my dad grew up in Israel and I was born there.*

Gary: I never would have guessed.

Gil: *I wouldn't expect you to — I came to the States when I was a few months old. For all intents and purposes, Garrison Keillor and I look and sound like Minnesotans — because we are. We both like camping, fishing, and have agonized over the Minnesota Vikings losing four*

"…survival just for survival's sake has never been a very good reason to be Jewish to me."

Super Bowls. Unlike Garrison, though, I have no Lake Woebegone in my background. What I have is more like Jewish woe. My dad was born in Europe, and both my parents had large numbers of aunts, uncles, cousins, and other relatives who died in the Holocaust. Between that and Israel, being Jewish has always been an important part of me. Still, like you, survival just for survival's sake has never been a very good reason to be Jewish to me. Then about when I turned 30, I met a rabbi who said to me, "What are you going to tell your kids when they are teenagers and they say, 'Dad, why should we be Jewish anyway?'"

Gary: What did you say?

Gil: *I hemmed and hawed and came up with some kind of weak answer that I don't even remember. I do remember that I knew at that moment that, for myself, I needed and wanted to find an answer that was better than to avenge Hitler. I also realized that I wanted my kids to be Jewish, but beyond that I was not sure why. My recollection is that the only answer I could come up with was that somehow Judaism had lasted thousands of years — even though I had trouble finding meaning in it for today. So maybe...*

Gary: So maybe the time has come for it to evolve out of history.

Gil: *Well, I did wonder: Maybe Judaism's time has come — and gone? But before I jumped to that conclusion, I knew that over the centuries, Jews much smarter than I am must have asked many of my same questions. After all, modern philosophies, sciences, and forms of government didn't begin in the last 10 years. A lot of people must have concluded that Judaism does have meaning or it would not have survived to this day.*

Gary: How can you be so sure?

Gil: *I wasn't sure, but I decided that before I passed on or junked Judaism, I owed it to myself, my kids, and all of the people who preserved Judaism for centuries to at least investigate. In other words, before the garbage truck made its pickup, I wanted to be sure I understood what I was throwing away.*

Gary: What do you mean by "investigate"?

Gil: *For me it has meant asking a lot of questions and taking classes. It has also meant reading. Luckily — though I now realize it's not luck — there are a lot of wonderful people and books with good answers. That's not to say I've found all the answers I'm looking for — I expect I'll have questions until my dying day. But for the most part, I've found answers to many of my questions about Judaism that I'm comfortable with.*

Gary: Like what?

Gil: *Like I think Judaism does have meaning. I understand why I want Judaism for me and my kids.*

Gary: Really? That's nice to hear. Then it's my turn to ask you, how are you defining Judaism?

> **"I think it's racist thinking that Jews should only marry Jews — that's repulsive to me."**

Gil: *The best I can come up with is that Judaism is a way of life.*

Gary: Come on, that's it? The result of all your questioning? You have got to have more to say than that. Whole books have been written on the subject.

Gil: *Elaborating on what I said is easy, but still, what I said is the simplest and best definition I've come up with: Judaism is a way of life. It's more than a religion and it's not a race.*

Gary: In that case, you had better elaborate a little.

Gil: *Most of what I've read says that the Jewish way of life or if you prefer, the Jewish way of living revolves around three areas. I call them E.S.P.*

Gary: E.S.P.?

Gil: *That's right. The E stands for ethics. The S stands for spirituality and the P stands for peoplehood. One famous Jewish thinker described them as: behaving, believing, and belonging. Within the Jewish tradition, each component of our E.S.P. is sacred.*

Gary: If they're all sacred, how is this different from what I said, that Judaism is a religion?

Gil: *It's different for a couple of reasons. First, to say that Judaism is a religion is far too limited a definition, because Jews are supposed to act and live ethically regardless of whether or not they have faith in God.*

Gary: What about being a race? By the way, I think it's racist thinking that Jews should only marry Jews — that's repulsive to me.

Gil: *It would be repulsive to me too — if Judaism was a race. Lots of people think Jews are a race. Anti-Semites love to call us a race — but it's simply not true. A person of any color can be a Jew — just look at a city street in Israel to confirm that. Anyone can become a member of the Jewish people — otherwise how could people convert to Judaism? You can't convert to being a Caucasian or any other race. You can be born a Jew or you can choose to become a Jew, but it has nothing to do with what you look like. Maybe what throws people is that one of the three "sacred" parts of being Jewish is to think of other Jews as family members — again regardless of your or their faith in God.*

Gary: I'm confused. You keep using the word *sacred*. It sounds like you're saying Judaism is not a religion and it is a religion.

Gil: *I'm saying that Judaism is a religion and more. Maybe I should be more clear about the word* sacred. *In our tradition, Jewish ethics, spirituality, and peoplehood are each deeply respected and revered. Each is considered greater than us. What's confusing is that they each stand alone and they are also connected to each other.*

Gary: How can they stand alone and also be connected?

Gil: *That's a fair question. I played with this problem on paper and came up with this diagram and definition that explains what I mean. This is how I define Judaism: Judaism is a way of life consisting of these three separate sacred components: E.S.P. — ethics, spirituality, and peoplehood. They overlap like this... like the Olympic rings.*

Judaism = A Way of Life
Consisting of E.S.P.:

Gary: I think I'm tracking with you, but you'd better say a bit more.

Gil: *At first glance, this might seem complicated, but it's really not. It's like three interlocking pieces of art. Each piece or circle stands alone. Together, they add to each other's beauty. I think of it as richness. Judaism gives you a lot of wonderful options for finding meaning. At least it does for me.*

Gary: Like what?

Gil: *You can choose to enter the Jewish way of life through any of these circles. And from each circle you can access the other two circles. You can even spend most of your time in one of these circles and still be considered a Jew.*

Gary: What do you mean?

Gil: *Well, today I think most Jews most easily sense their Jewishness in the peoplehood circle. In other words, by feeling that they belong to a people or a community. Even the most unaffiliated Jews seem to feel this sense of belonging if there is a hint of anti-Semitism in the air.*

Gary: I agree with that, especially if the anti-Semitism is widely publicized or comes from the mouth of someone famous, or if the subject of the Holocaust comes up.

Gil: *Even without anti-Semitism, I think the peoplehood circle is the easiest to access and to find some meaning for yourself. But there are still two other circles. You can find meaning in the Jewish code of ethical behavior — like how Jews are supposed to treat a disadvantaged person — or as your parents used to say, "the Jewish thing to do." Finally, and the hardest for me, you can also find it through your belief or spiritual searching.*

"Even the most unaffiliated Jews seem to feel this sense of belonging if there is a hint of anti-Semitism in the air."

Gary: Let me get straight what you're saying. You're saying that the Jewish way of life consists of any or all three of the E.S.P. components: ethics, spirituality, and community, or as you put it, "peoplehood." This sounds both simple and complicated.

Gil: *The simple part is that in Judaism there are just three components, as you said. The complex part is that you can choose to emphasize or deemphasize any or all of the three and still be considered a Jew. Plus, because the circles intersect and overlap, you can end up with a number of combinations that give Judaism meaning.*

Gary: I'm not following you. Give me an example.

Gil: *Okay. For me, directly entering the spirituality circle is a challenging thing to do. It's hard for me to understand and relate to God. On the other hand, I have an easy time entering the peoplehood circle. I mean, it's easy for me to feel I belong to the Jewish people. Sometimes, through my feeling of belonging to the Jewish people, I can also access the spirituality circle. A good example is attending a large Jewish rally or community celebration. For me, there is often an aura about these gatherings that is powerful and beyond explaining. To me it feels spiritual.*

Gary: Maybe that's part of the chain of Judaism I was talking about.

Gil: *Could be. Here, I'll give you a different kind of example — this one about the ethics circle. Judaism says we're supposed to do nice things for other people — like visit someone who's sick. Even though I certainly do not enjoy going to the hospital or, worse yet, a nursing home to see a friend or relative, something about making the effort is uplifting—at times I'd even call it spiritual. And if I am visiting a Jewish nursing home, I can also feel that I am part of the people-hood circle. I can feel all three circles overlapping.*

Gary: So are you saying that peoplehood or ethics can lead to spirituality?

Gil: *Depending on the person, they might. My point is that, alone or together, they are each considered sacred. Plus, they each can lead to or overlap one or both of the other two circles. Alone or together they can provide meaning. Like remember I said that in a way chopped liver is Judaism?*

Gary: I remember I didn't know what you meant then, and I still don't.

Gil: *Chopped liver is part of our peoplehood, part of our culture, part of the way Jews as a people do things. Of course, it's just a little part — a little part of the all-encompassing three intersecting circles that form the Jewish way of life.*

Gary: I wouldn't call chopped liver meaningful.

Gil: *Neither would I — by itself. But each little part contributes to the Jewish way of life, like a mosaic. It might take a little imagination, but I can find meaning in the small parts. For me, it takes no imagination to find meaning in the three large components that make up Judaism. In fact, the more I look at Judaism, the more I find for my life.*

Gary: That's nice — for you. I'm not sure I care to look so much. I don't have a need to get to where you are with your Judaism. My life seems quite fulfilling and meaningful the way it is, not to mention busy. Plus, I don't think Judaism is the only answer.

Gil: *Judaism is definitely not the only answer. I won't even say it's the best answer. But I will say, I've found that it's a good answer — a very good answer. An answer with a proven and amazing track record of making a positive difference in the world — and it belongs to us, it's ours. You certainly don't have to pursue Judaism if you don't want to. But you did say that you are struggling over what to give your kids.*

Gary: That is true, and perhaps now I can at least provide them with a definition of Judaism. But I'm still not sure I would feel comfortable passing that on since I still have many other unresolved questions and issues about Judaism.

Key Points to Hold Onto

Chapter 2: "What Is Judaism Anyway?"

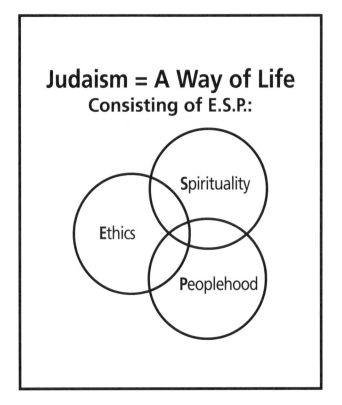

Judaism = A Way of Life
Consisting of E.S.P.:

- Each circle is sacred in Judaism.
- You can enter any of the circles to access the other two.
- You can find yourself Jewishly in one circle, or where they overlap.

Afterthoughts

The strongest reaction I heard from readers of this book when it was in manuscript form was positive feedback about the E.S.P. circles in this chapter. The gist of the comments was: "I finally understand what Judaism is, thanks to those circles."

One of the goals of the circles, and indeed this whole book, is to show that, regardless of your level of Jewish practice, understanding, or knowledge, there are a number of ways to enter Judaism. To underscore this goal, the next four chapters are organized using the circles. Chapters 3 and 4 focus on the spirituality circle — the most difficult circle to access for the majority of the Jews who spoke to me. Chapter 5 concentrates on peoplehood, and chapter 6 examines the ethics circle.

Readers of the manuscript told me that organizing the book using the circles was helpful to them. I hope it is for you as well. Several of those readers asked me how the circle diagram makes Judaism any different from any of the other great religions. There are several responses. First, the diagram is designed to show simply what Judaism is — not to show how Judaism is different from other religions. This book does not try to be a course in comparative religion.

That point aside, though, Judaism is different. There are differences from other religions within each of the circles. From what I have learned, the biggest difference may be the peoplehood circle itself. An example I have given much thought to is the tragic assassination of Israeli Prime Minister Yitzhak Rabin.

Many Jews, and even the general media, expressed shock that a Jew killed a fellow Jew. To me, that shock says something about Jews as a people. I have never heard that kind of shock expressed when a Moslem killed another Moslem or a Christian killed another Christian. Why? I believe the main reason is the uniqueness and sacredness of peoplehood in Judaism. But I am getting ahead of myself — the chapter on Jewish peoplehood is later in this book. As you can see, each of the circles offers plenty to think about.

Another important comment I heard about the circles was from a woman who told me she felt like going to her mother with the diagram and saying, "See, Mom, I am still Jewish, even if I don't go to synagogue." She also volunteered, however, that she realized she could use the diagram to "wimp out" on or rationalize her Judaism. "For example," she joked, tongue in cheek, "I could say I have Jewish relatives, so I qualify for the peoplehood circle, therefore I am Jewish. I know that's not a legitimate thing to say," she said. "So, seriously," she asked me, "what level of Judaism is really practicing Judaism?"

As I mentioned in my introductory comments to you, I am not attempting to answer that question for you in this book. Further, I do not want any of the thoughts contained in these afterthought sections (or anywhere in the book, for that matter) to be perceived as preachy or heavy-handed. Instead, please receive these thoughts as my personal point of view, which I offer for your consideration.

In answer to the question, what is a "correct" level of Judaism?, I respond by saying that this is a personal decision everyone makes for him- or herself. You can answer that question for yourself far better than I can. I hope you find some ideas in upcoming chapters that help you answer the "correct level" question for yourself. I would only suggest following Shakespeare's advice: "To thine own self be true."

Questions From This Chapter You May Wish to Ponder

- Where do you usually find yourself on the E.S.P. circles that make up the Jewish way of life?

- Have you found comfort or discomfort in the different circles? Why?

Chapter 3
"I'm Not Even Sure I Believe in God"

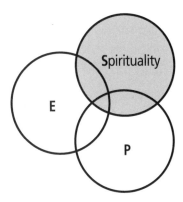

Broaching the subject of God is something most Jews don't seem to do very often. Few people (except children) would ask another person, "Do you believe in God?" After all, when was the last time you had an open discussion with another person — even a close friend — about God? I think many would find such a discussion socially awkward and even rude. In our society, it's almost as if sex is an easier topic to talk about. It seems most Jews consider faith to be a very private matter.

However, when I asked people to share their thoughts about God, they seemed anxious to speak to me about the subject. Speaking about God and spirituality consumed a large percentage of the time in many of the discussions I had. Several people told me this was the first time in many years that they had candidly discussed God with anyone. As the floodgates opened, I got the impression that unfortunately, silence on the subject of God is the case for many — even though they have a desire to reveal their thoughts. Perhaps the reason those who spoke to me shared so much is that they knew that everything they said would be held in confidence. Or perhaps people felt comfortable because we often spoke in terms of spirituality as opposed to using the word God. I have a suspicion that a big reason was simply because I asked and was willing to listen.

Whatever the reasons, I often heard two sentiments expressed. First, many (though certainly not all) almost seemed to want to talk about their doubts about God. Second, many expressed that Judaism was not addressing their spiritual needs.

In this chapter, you will get a flavor of these and the other issues I heard about God and spirituality. You may be comforted to learn that you're not the only one who has doubts. In addition, you'll see that spiritual questioning is very Jewish and does not make you a "bad" Jew. There are also thoughts in this chapter and the next about how Judaism might speak to you spiritually.

Rob

When Rob was a teenager, he said that he was such a complete misfit and mischief maker in religious school that he was thrown out. Then, in an attempt to "rehabilitate" him, he and three other "screwball" students were given a private education from the rabbi at his temple. They studied "Sex and What Judaism Had to Say About It." Rob loved not only the subject of sex ("I was a teenager, after all"), but also the way the rabbi integrated Judaism into the subject. That class, however, was his only contact with the rabbi, and when it ended, so did his Jewish education and virtually any formal association with Judaism for the rest of his life.

"My rabbi would probably be surprised to learn that I ended up becoming an ob/gyn. On the other hand, maybe he wouldn't be surprised."

Rob is 37 and has ambivalent feelings about being Jewish because he has such a hard time believing in God. Being a doctor has furthered his difficulty with the idea of God. On the one hand, seeing "the miracle" of birth so often makes him wonder about a God and creator. On the other hand, "being a person schooled in the sciences and who relies on empirical data" makes thinking of God the creator "seem like a giant fairy tale."

With this ambivalence, he said, come simultaneous contradictory feelings of being ashamed and not ashamed of his questions about God. He mentioned that our discussion was probably the first time in decades that he had seriously spoken to anyone about his thoughts and feelings about God. He added, "That's sad, especially since I enjoyed this discussion — it was kind of a relief to express my doubts."

Rob: To tell you the truth, I'm not even sure I believe in God.

Gil: *Do you think that makes you unique?*

Rob: Maybe… I guess I'm not sure. I might even be an atheist. I'm probably more of an agnostic—deep down. I'm not sure if people invented God or vice versa. I do know that all of this doubt makes me feel like I'm not much of a Jew.

Gil: *Why?*

Rob: Are you kidding? Here I am not sure I believe in God, and I have to ask, "What kind of Jew am I?" Feeling this uncertain about God, it's hard for me to take much of Judaism very seriously. If I go to the synagogue, I open up the prayer book and I ask myself, "Who am I praying to? Who or what is this God? I can't relate to this." And the rituals and the laws, even the few things I occasionally do — like when I go to a Passover seder — I find I'm asking myself, "What am I doing here anyway?" I feel like a complete hypocrite.

Gil: *So for you, being unsure or ambivalent about God is a nonstarter. If your faith in God is at best a question, everything about Judaism feels like hypocrisy or a waste of time.*

Rob: Let me put it this way, I'm not a religious or observant person. I'm not into Jewish ritual, prayer, or the temple. I have a hard time going forward with religion or observance feeling as I do about God. I sure don't feel like much of a Jew.

Gil: *What would you say if I told you that you're very much a Jew?*

Rob: I'd say, "What do you mean?" In fact, I think I'll say that. What do you mean?

Gil: *Your questions about faith are not unique — they are very Jewish. I say that based on my own personal experience of having some of the same questions. When I began to look for answers, I was pleasantly shocked to find that I was not alone. For thousands of years, Jews have struggled with many of the same questions.*

Rob: Great, so they were also lousy Jews.

Gil: *That was my first reaction too. I used to think that having doubts about God made me a bad Jew. But I've learned that that's a misconception about Judaism. Judaism cares a lot more about a person's behavior than about their belief. But after exploring this business of faith, I now understand why most Jews don't know this.*

Rob: What do you mean?

Gil: *I came up with a phenomenon that explains this. I call it the "Christianization of Judaism."*

Rob: What in the world is that supposed to mean?

Gil: *In Christianity, if you don't believe in Christ, you're not a Christian. End of discussion. But in Judaism, not having faith in God does not disqualify you from being a Jew. On top of that, questioning about God is very much a part of our tradition. Our name is very different from "Christian," which is literally a believer in Christ — or for that matter, "Muslim," which comes from the Arabic word for "submission" — to God's will.*

Rob: So we're called Jews, so what?

Gil: *We're also called the people Israel. The word* Israel *in Hebrew means wrestler or struggler with God. So if you struggle with questions about God, you're living up to your namesake: You're a member of the people Israel. You're doing something that is very Jewish. But living in societies dominated by gentiles, many of us Jews have picked up the idea that if we have questions about faith, that makes us bad Jews. It just isn't so.*

Rob: There is something comforting in that.

Gil: *It was to me. I found something else that made me feel even more comfortable that I think you, too, will appreciate. I had a teacher once who told me to stop calling myself and others good or bad Jews. He had a much better idea.*

> **"I used to think that having doubts about God made me a bad Jew. But I've learned that that's a misconception..."**

Rob: I'm listening.

Gil: *He said to use the term* serious *Jew. Serious Jews are people who actively struggle with their Judaism. I think being actively serious is good.*

Rob: I like that. I have often thought of myself as a second-class Jew. I mean, I don't really practice any Jewish ritual or often go to temple. Actually, inside I probably think of myself as a bad Jew — though somehow that doesn't seem right.

Gil: *I think judging a person's Jewishness by how many times they pray or perform ritual is dangerous. Better to me is to think in terms of a seriousness continuum. On one end is active; on the other end is passive. To me, actively being serious or struggling with my Judaism is a place I feel good about.*

Rob: I like that much better than calling myself a good or bad Jew, and I'm feeling actively serious now. But I can't believe many rabbis would buy your idea about faith. Are you telling me that rabbis are not sure they believe in God?

Gil: *I've never polled rabbis, but I have spoken to rabbis who have told me that they have had doubts about God at different points in their adult lives. I'd like to talk more about that, but first can I ask you: When you say you're not sure you believe in God, what exactly are you calling God?*

Rob: It's easier for me to tell you what I don't believe in. I don't believe in a God who is an old grandfather figure with a long white beard who is pulling puppet strings and intervening in my life or the world. All I need to do is look at the Holocaust or all of the other evil in the world to destroy that God idea. The Holocaust was so horrible, how could you not question if there is a God — and if there is, what kind of God allows such evil to happen?

> **"One daughter of Holocaust survivors told me that her father regained his faith in God because the Holocaust taught him that he could not believe in people."**

Gil: *I don't know.*

Rob: That's it? Don't you have any better answers?

Gil: *Hey, I'm just a person. I don't have any voodoo or on-line connection to God. I wish I did. In the meantime, I have to rely on a low-tech solution — I have to guess. Also, I read other people's answers.*

Rob: So what do they say?

Gil: *To me some of the most thought-provoking answers have come from Holocaust survivors. After all, these are the people who actually experienced the atrocities of the Nazis. Some survivors never were able to accept the notion of God again. Yet others did. Survivors have different answers. One daughter of Holocaust survivors told me that her father regained his faith in God because the Holocaust taught him that he could not believe in people.*

Rob: Hmmm, that's a powerful answer.

Gil: *I thought so. Another survivor I heard had a similar answer. Her explanation was that God is not a baby-sitter. The Holocaust was the work of humanity.*

Rob: Now that you bring these explanations up, I remember in high school reading the book *Night* by Elie Wiesel; he was also a survivor. There is a haunting scene about a boy who is being hanged by the Nazis in front of the other inmates and someone shouts out, "Where is God?" And Wiesel answers, "God is up there on the gallows." I was never sure if that meant that God was dead or that God was suffering along with the victims of the Holocaust.

Gil: *That's a good question. I don't know either. An answer I have heard about God suffering with the victims is that God does not intervene to stop the evil of people. If we want goodness to prevail, then people must stop evil — when we do, God rejoices along with us.*

Rob: I think that last part is nonsense. The Allied army stopped the Holocaust, and God had nothing to do with it.

Gil: *At the same time, if you wanted, you could argue that God was on the side that ultimately won and prevailed over evil. I have heard the argument that the Jews were slaves in Egypt for 400 years before God rescued them. By comparison, World War II lasted only six years. Unfortunately, of course, there is no way to know or prove any of this with absolute certainty.*

Rob: It's hard for me to fathom what Holocaust survivors have gone through, and I'm really amazed that anyone could find faith after that. But for me, I guess those answers are just very difficult to accept. You know, you can take some of this rationale to the other extreme too. For example, I have heard of rabbis explaining that the Holocaust was a punishment God placed on the Jewish people for their misdeeds. I can't believe that. I have a friend whose family experienced a tragic accident that was random — it could have happened to anyone. When they asked a rabbi about it, he said something about it being God's will. They were badly hurt and alienated by that thinking. And I don't blame them. I just don't believe in a God like that.

Gil: *Well, is there something you do believe in?*

Rob: I guess I believe in nature somehow. When I see mountains or the ocean or even a nature program on television, I do feel a certain awe that is beyond words. I sense there is some force or a life force out there, and it's bigger than me. But I can't come up with an explanation beyond that. And I wonder whether we have made up this idea of God to make us feel more comfortable because we can't come up with any explanation for so much of what happens.

Gil: *What you just said reminds me of your question about rabbis believing in God. You should ask a few rabbis to explain to you what kind of God they believe in. You will probably be surprised by the answers. I was. And I emphasize the plural: answers. Within Judaism there have been many conceptions of God. There's even a book out today called* Finding God: Ten Jewish Responses.

Rob: Ten?

Gil: *It startled me too. I learned two main things from the book. First, within traditional Judaism, generally speaking, there is the belief that one God exists. The second thing is that there is a lot of uncertainty about what that God is. There are many thoughts and images of God within Judaism — so many that you can probably find some of the same questions and ideas about God that you share. I did. For example, one of the greatest rabbis and thinkers in Judaism — Maimonides (he was also called the Rambam) — believed that you can* only say what God is not. For example, he believed that God does not control the world, does not interfere in the workings of nature, and does not intervene to stop evil.

Rob: That sounds like something I might accept, but I'd need to hear more.

Gil: He had many thoughts about God. He also recognized that belief was hard for many. He compared belief to a horde of people around a castle trying to see the king. Some people believe there's a king inside, even though the size of the crowd prevents them from even seeing the gate. Others need to be in the castle to believe, and still others need to see the king to believe.

> **"I wonder whether we have made up this idea of God to make us feel more comfortable because we can't [explain] so much of what happens."**

Rob: Different levels of belief. I am probably on the skeptical side. It's very hard for me to feel certain about God.

Gil: Personally, I don't know how anyone can always feel certain. Plus if you think about it, Jews have always been prohibited from even making images of God. If people are prohibited from creating a concrete image of God, it's easy for me to see how this can result in a lot of uncertainty, questioning, and doubt. In a way, then, I think that every Jew is forced to come up with an individual concept of God — though we have a lot of traditional sources we can look to for guidance. Although even within our tradition there is disagreement. For example, there have been great Jewish thinkers who had conceptions of God that were different than Maimonides'.

Rob: Why hasn't anyone ever told me this before?

Gil: *Maybe because you never asked — at least that was the case for me. Until recently, I never asked anyone what Judaism says about God — or for that matter, what they think about God. A strange thing has happened in this modern "enlightened" time of ours: talking about sex today seems far less intimate or embarrassing than talking about God.*

Rob: I will admit, I'd feel kind of awkward bringing up "Do you believe in God?" in most settings. I sure wouldn't do it at work or at a party… maybe at a convenience store… just kidding. I'd almost be embarrassed to ask some of these questions of a rabbi. That just doesn't seem appropriate.

Gil: *If that's the case for you, then you could ask any knowledgeable Jew. I think a rabbi is one of the most appropriate people to ask. After all, they have the knowledge and the training to answer. But people seldom ask rabbis or anyone else — I can only guess why. Maybe people are intimidated because they think rabbis have such strong faith. Or maybe in this science-based world, asking questions about God and spirituality, as you put it, feels awkward or embarrassing.*

Rob: That's true. We expect all of our answers today to be provable in the laboratory, or in survey or sales results. It seems that the answers we seek today should be measurable or logically explained.

Gil: *I think you're right. Yet everyone knows that we can't explain everything with pure data. Still, somehow we want to be able to see God if we look through a microscope somewhere. But dealing with issues of the spirit, spirituality, our innermost thoughts and souls is not science — it's much closer to art.*

Rob: Then why are we taught as kids such simplistic and black-and-white ideas about God, miracles, and God appearing to our ancestors? For example, I was a kid when my grandmother passed away, and I remember hearing over and over about how God was now taking care of Grandma and that I didn't need to worry about her being sick anymore. Like God was some kind of person.

Gil: *That was probably because you and I and all kids ask tough questions of our parents. Like about the death of a grandparent, or about tornadoes, earthquakes, and accidents. We give kids answers because they need comforting. I think we give simple answers because we think kids won't understand or because we're not sure of the answers ourselves. After all, how would you answer your children if they were very upset and asked you, "Why did Grandma die?"*

Rob: I see your point, but what about the Bible? The way God is portrayed: He appears, He intervenes, He makes miracles happen, He's a He... The Bible is always using human attributes to describe God, like angry, jealous, merciful. How do you explain all of that?

Gil: *I'd explain it the same way I explained what we tell kids. In truth, we adults tend to speak to each other about God using the same terms we use when we talk to children — I think for the same two reasons: First, we're struggling for answers ourselves, and second, we use language and images that we can understand or at least partially grasp.*

Rob: I still don't see how anyone can accept the way the Bible speaks about God. In this day and age, it's just so unbelievable — at least to me.

Gil: *You're not the only one. This reminds me of a joke I heard about a kid who came home from Sunday school, and his dad asked him what he had learned. He said, "Dad, it was*

> **"How can you expect modern, educated people to believe Bible stories and descriptions?"**

so cool — we learned that the Israelites were stuck in front of the Red Sea and the Egyptian army was rushing to kill them. Then the Israeli Army Corps of Engineers appeared and quickly built pontoon bridges and they all crossed over. Then when the Egyptians tried to cross, the Israeli Air Force came and bombed the bridges and all the

Israelites escaped." And his dad said, "I don't believe they really taught you that story." And the son said, "You're right, Dad, but if I told you what they really taught us, you would never believe that story."

Rob: That's not bad, and I agree with that kid. How can you expect modern, educated people to believe Bible stories and descriptions?

Gil: *I think your question is very fair. From what I've read, the rabbis over the centuries thought about the same issue and came up with an explanation. They said that the Bible was written in the language of humans, so that the people could understand the complex thoughts found in the words. The rabbis also pointed out that the Bible is full of metaphor and poetic language, so we often need to look beyond the actual words to find meaning and understanding. They also said that the Bible has 70 faces; every time you look at it you may see a different face or interpretation.*

Rob: Those are some creative explanations by the rabbis, but it sounds to me like some rationalizations.

Gil: *I can see why you might say that, but I think the rabbis' explanation makes sense. I'll give you an example from another walk of life. My neighbor is a doctor. He told me that a patient from India came to see him. The patient complained through a translator that he thought he was having a heart attack. My neighbor asked him all the routine questions: "Do you have pain in your left arm? Do you feel weight on your chest?" and so on. The answer to each question was "no, no, no." So my neighbor was about to send him home. Then the translator said, "Doctor, my friend says to tell you that he feels as if an elephant is sitting on his chest." With this, my neighbor immediately admitted the patient, who, sure enough, was having a heart attack.*

Rob: You mean to tell me that asking about elephants is not part of your neighbor's standard protocol of questions? He sounds like a malpractice suit in the making.

Gil: *You've now picked up a little tip in case you ever decide to practice medicine in India. As for America, that's a true story that I think shows how important the choice of language and metaphors is for understanding. That's what I think the rabbis meant when they said that the Bible was written in simple human language so humans would understand.*

Rob: Okay, I can accept that argument about the language in the Bible. But what about today? How are we supposed to get past simple understandings of God when rabbis, teachers, and most other adults still use simple descriptions of God?

Gil: *Well, I said that we "tend" to use this kind of language. Not all adults use those kinds of descriptions. But you still raise a valid point. I think part of the answer is that the level of the discussion is raised by all who participate in the discussion. Today, we seem to look for quick 20-second "sound bite" answers to our questions.*

Rob: So you think attention spans are shorter today than they used to be?

Gil: *I'm no expert on attention spans. Maybe what has changed is our willingness to talk about the subject of God. As you said earlier, bringing up the subjects of God, faith, and belief is awkward or even embarrassing. I think a lot of people would agree with you.*

Rob: Are you saying that I should be prepared for a long, heavy discussion if I want some answers about God?

Gil: *I wouldn't put it that way exactly. Instead, I'd say that the subject is complex and there is no one certain answer. Some people spend many years of their lives wrestling with a concept of God that they can feel comfortable with... reading, talking to other people, exploring... but this spiritual search can also be enjoyable.*

Rob: What's enjoyable about it?

Gil: *I find this discussion enjoyable, for example. I don't think it's embarrassing. I think it's interesting.*

Rob: It is rather personal, but I must say it is stimulating.

Gil: *For me, I find making discoveries is fun. There can be joy in learning new things and in finding that other people share my views or even disagree. Plus I enjoy making discoveries and learning new things with other people. It's also nice to find out that you're not alone in your searching. Usually for me, the whole process of talking to other people about spirituality and God is stimulating. And, at the risk of sounding a little bit like a nut, sometimes I even find it comforting and uplifting.*

Rob: I don't think that sounds nutty, but what happens if you find other people who are looking and looking and just decide they are so lost that the search is not worth it anymore?

Gil: *Sometimes I can feel that way all by myself — that's when I really need other people. I found a great story about that from a 19th-century European rabbi. He said that a man was lost for days in the forest when he ran into someone else. He asked, "Can you show me the way?" The other guy said, "I'm lost also. But I can tell you, do not go where I have been — that leads nowhere. Let's search for the way together."*

> **"The conclusion I've reached... is that, within Jewish tradition, knowing about God with certainty is humanly impossible."**

Rob: I like that analogy, but wouldn't searching alone or with someone else include looking at other religions' concepts of God and spirituality?

Gil: *It could and does for some Jews. I've spoken to a number who have. A funny thing happens to some of these people. As they explore other faiths, they often find Judaism shares many of the same beliefs — they just didn't know that before. And they like the Jewish concepts.*

Rob: Come on, you mean to tell me that Judaism's concept of God is the same as, say, Hinduism or Buddhism?

Gil: *No, Judaism does differ from other religions — but many distinctions are not black and white. Like I was saying before, within Judaism there is a vast variety of opinions and thoughts about God and spirituality. The conclusion I've reached from this is that, within Jewish tradition, knowing about God with certainty is humanly impossible. This is the conclusion that many great Jewish thinkers and rabbis have come to.*

Rob: I'm not clear on what that has to do with other faiths.

Gil: *My point is that, because of this uncertainty, you find a wide range of Jewish opinions. Within this range, you can find Jewish concepts that are compatible with other faiths. For example, I wanted to see why some Jews have been attracted to Native American spirituality. The Native American concept of God is often referred to as "The Great Spirit." But I learned that in the language of the Sioux Indians, the term for God, Wakan Tanka, can be translated as "The Great Mystery."*

Rob: How is this compatible with Judaism?

Gil: *Traditional Sioux Indians believe that humans cannot understand such a vast mystery as God and they disapprove of arguing over the exactness of God. It's one of the reasons they resented missionaries, by the way. In our Talmud, our great collection of Jewish law, there's a story about an emperor who approaches a rabbi and says, "I want to see your God." The rabbi tells him to stare at the sun. The emperor says, "I can't do that." To which the rabbi replies, "If you can't even look at the sun, which is just one of God's ministers, how do you expect to see God?"*

Rob: So the rabbi is saying that humans cannot comprehend God?

Gil: *That's the way I interpret the story. And it's also the way I'd interpret the Native American concept of "The Great Mystery."*

Rob: So what does all this say about searching for spirituality?

Gil: *I'd say two things. First, I think the search is full of discovery that can be enjoyable. Second, I've found that our tradition is rich. There is enough there to keep you exploring for a lifetime. You can look elsewhere if you want, but I think you should at least include our tradition in your searching. Just as a tease, I'll throw in that if you want a real eye-opening experience, take a look at Jewish mysticism or Kabbalah while you explore spirituality. The Kabbalah is said to reveal the secrets of the universe and God. You may be intrigued by Kabbalah's ten Divine Spheres, including a feminine notion of God.*

Rob: I am intrigued, but I've got to tell you there is nothing spiritual for me about doing any of this searching at the synagogue. The synagogue is not a place I go to access God or spirituality.

Gil: *Where do you go?*

Rob: I remember as a kid trying to "find God" — it didn't work.

Gil: *What happened?*

Rob: Actually, I was trying to see if God could find me. I was skipping out of Hebrew school, and I hid for a long time. I figured God is supposed to see everything. He's got to be watching me cutting class and he will send me a signal.

"Why does Judaism insist that you have to find God at the synagogue, anyway?"

Gil: *And?*

Rob: Perhaps the signal was boredom. I got so bored I went back to class and spent the rest of the day goofing around with my friends — that's probably the closest I've ever come to having a religious experience at religious school.

Gil: *But now you're an adult, and you say you don't access spirituality at the synagogue. So, where do you go?*

Rob: I don't think I go anywhere. I'm not sure I think about it very consciously either, but things do happen to me from time to time that are spiritual.

Gil: *Like what?*

Rob: There are actually many things. Like when my kids were born. I cried… I was just overwhelmed. I had to say there's got to be something bigger than me here. At the time, my wife said for her it was painkillers. But seriously, there are things — like when I deliver a baby — that seem miraculous to me — when I can't explain what I'm experiencing. Like I said, nature is like that. Seeing a mountain. Or even little things, like some mornings when the grass is first cut. Sometimes I look at my fingers and I can't believe they work the way they do. I often marvel at the way the body heals from surgery. And I know this is going to sound mushy and sentimental, but I also feel it when I see a great movie and someone falls in love. That, to me, is spirituality. Or I read in the paper that someone has the inspiration or superhuman patience to invent something mind-boggling and fantastic like a gene therapy for some medical problem… I also know that I've felt something bigger than me during dark times… like when my mother was dying. That was… I don't know… Now that you have pushed me, I guess I often have a feeling that I'd say feels spiritual.

Gil: *Exactly what do you mean by feeling spiritual?*

Rob: As I said, it's hard to put into words, but the closest I could come would be that I feel awed, amazed, attuned to how mysterious and unbelievable things are. When things are bad, I feel alone and frightened. When things are good, I feel grateful beyond words. There, that's what spirituality feels like to me. Now maybe you understand why the synagogue doesn't work for me. None of these feelings come up at the synagogue for me. Why does Judaism insist that you have to find God at the synagogue, anyway?

Gil: *Let me react by asking you to react to something. Tell me what you think of this prayer from one of the Eastern religions. It goes something like this: "May it be my custom to go outdoors each day among the trees and grasses, among all growing things, and there may I be alone and enter into prayer to talk with the one that I belong to."*

Rob: My reaction is that, in general, I like it. This is what's missing from Judaism. I wouldn't have guessed it's Eastern, though. I would have said that it came from California. Not really. I would have guessed that it was Native American because it seems so connected to nature and the Earth.

Gil: *No, it's Eastern all right. The Eastern religion this prayer comes from is Eastern European — Judaism. It's a prayer from one of the greatest rabbis of the last few centuries; his name was Rabbi Nachman of Bratzlav.*

Rob: Wait a minute, are you telling me that a rabbi was advocating praying outside among the trees and not in a synagogue?

Gil: *I suspect this rabbi would say to pray both places. All I'm trying to do is respond to your comment about Judaism insisting on finding God only in the synagogue. That is far from Jewish thinking... Judaism says that there are many places to find God and to try and connect with that spirituality. For thousands of years, Judaism has emphasized that nature is one of those places. And so is your bed, when you lie down and when you get up, and when you eat, work, and play — countless places. A few minutes ago, you told me the many places you have experienced spirituality. Your experiences are consistent with Judaism's thinking about spirituality.*

Rob: I'm not sure I understand.

Gil: *What I mean is that when it comes to spirituality and God, Judaism says specifics are hard or impossible to describe. But in general, our tradition says there is something greater than humans. Call it God, call it a life force, call it the spirit in your soul or spirituality. What to call "it" is difficult — but we know it when we feel it. Nature is one of the places where many people feel it — that there is something greater than humans. But just as you described, you can feel the awe of spirituality everywhere. Judaism says the same thing.*

Rob: But if I want to feel that awe, I've got nature to remind me. Why do I need Judaism?

Gil: *I think that is a great question. One answer I've come up with is that there is a lot more to Judaism than spirituality. Even if the idea of God is difficult to accept, Judaism still offers ethics and peoplehood. As for me, I have found that the Jewish concept of spirituality makes sense. When I feel lost, it helps me feel less lost. And I really like the idea that my questions and searching are kosher — so to speak. It's okay; in fact, it's very Jewish.*

Rob: My doubts and questioning are okay. I like that too. I've never felt very confident in my faith in God, but I think I've always kind of believed that there is some kind of indefinable force in the world that is greater than me. After all, I don't think I created myself. But I must say I never knew that my vague concept could be considered acceptable by Judaism. There's something appealing and comforting in all this.

Gil: *I was also comforted when I learned what Judaism says about God. I now think that I was being too hard on myself by calling myself a nonreligious bad Jew. I was not terribly observant, that was true — but now I realize that by searching for spirituality and questioning about God, I'm being a serious Jew. I think searching and being serious is good.*

Rob: For me, "finding spirituality" isn't easy to do. As I said, the times I have found it, I wasn't really looking for it. But I do often wrestle with my many doubts and questions. This idea of being an actively serious Jew is new to me. It does seem to be a constructive and positive way to think about myself as I struggle.

Key Points to Hold Onto

Chapter 3: "I'm Not Even Sure I Believe in God"

- Jews are called the people Israel. *Israel* means "wrestle with God."

- Having doubts and questioning the nature of God is very Jewish.

- Rather than "good" or "bad" Jew, think in terms of "seriousness." Serious Jews actively wrestle with their Judaism.

- While Judaism believes in one God, there is great uncertainty within our tradition as to "a" definition of God.

- Looking for quick, simplistic explanations of God in Judaism is unrealistic (notwithstanding the fact that we tend to give kids simple explanations). Still, the search can be enjoyable.

- Judaism definitely recognizes that spirituality can be found outside of the synagogue. Nature is one example.

Afterthoughts

The first time I heard the idea of being a "serious" Jew (in a class taught by Dennis Prager), I immediately found value and comfort in the concept. Many people who read this chapter expressed a similar reaction to me. However, in one of the focus groups I held with people who had read the manuscript, some of the participants said that, in their opinion, "serious" was not good enough. They said that if you think seriously but never act, then you're not really being serious. Their point seemed valid to me, so I modified the concept in the dialogue and in my head, to strive to be an "actively serious" Jew.

Another point people commented to me about was whether a person could really be Jewish if their faith was weak or nonexistent. They wondered how a rabbi would react to that idea. In response, I cited a story told by Rabbi Harold Kushner in his book *To Life*. Rabbi Kushner writes that when he was a student in rabbinical school, a professor asked the class to name the ten greatest Jewish figures of the 20th century. They wrote names like Freud, Einstein, Theodore Herzl, and other great scientists, writers, and statesmen. When they had finished, the professor said, "Now, next to the person's name, list the synagogue he attended each week." The professor's and Kushner's point in telling this story was that the Jewish world and even these rabbinical students considered these figures to be great Jews — but not because of their Jewish faith or religious observance.

Finally, some have asked me how I define spirituality and how I define God. First, I must say that I am not a theologian, nor is this book a philosophical examination of deity. Still, the question is fair. In keeping with Jewish tradition, I say that I constantly struggle for answers. To me, God and spirituality deal with matters of the spirit, matters of conscience, matters of the soul. They are matters that are beyond my comprehension and are bigger than I am.

I will go out on a limb and say that I think there is such a thing as the human soul (even though I would have a hard time explaining what that is to my kids, or to an adult, for that matter). I also think that human souls need spiritual nourishment. I will also take the risk of putting in writing my belief that our souls can receive strength, comfort, and guidance from a source greater than we are that defies explanation. How does that happen? Does that really happen? Did I and others make all of this up so we could feel more comfortable with our mortality or smallness? I don't know. I continue to grapple.

The conclusion or conclusions you reach about God and spirituality are your business and are difficult or impossible to prove. Still, I hope you have seen in this chapter that while Judaism maintains the concept of one God, struggling with our spirituality, a definition of God, and the many questions that are a part of this mystery is very, very Jewish.

Many told me that they experience little or no spiritual sustenance and struggle at the synagogue or temple, or through prayer. The next chapter takes a closer look at these complaints.

Questions From This Chapter You May Wish to Ponder

- When it comes to God or spirituality, how would you articulate what you do and do not believe in?

- Would you be willing to honestly discuss your thoughts about God or spirituality with another person? Whom? Why?

- Do you consider yourself to be an actively serious Jew? Why or why not?

Chapter 4
"There's No Spirituality for Me in Synagogues and Prayer"

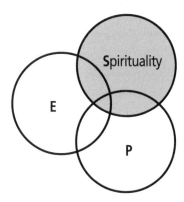

Many people told me that finding spirituality in Judaism was, to put it mildly, a challenge. The problem: The traditional Jewish modes of access to spirituality and God — namely, prayer, synagogues, temples, and rabbis — just don't reach or touch them.

I was able to relate to much of what I heard in this department. Over the years, I have tried (and continue to try) to have my spiritual needs met at services. I have been only partially successful.

Unfortunately, I heard from many who have experienced no success and have stopped trying. They told me that services offer them little or nothing that they consider spiritual or meaningful. To address these issues, Jewish institutions of spirituality have some demanding work ahead of them. Personally, I would like to see some significant changes.

But even as I say that, still I believe that Judaism today has much to offer spiritually. This chapter suggests ways you may find some spiritual nourishment through synagogues, temples, prayer, and rabbis.

Amy

Amy just had her third child and is thrilled. Her baby is a girl after two boys, and as she said, "At 43, there were not going to be any more tries." Her boys are four and seven. She's actually a little too thrilled, because her excitement has created a problem for her. When each of her babies was born, she was torn over whether to return to work as a successful advertising executive. Each time she lamented the time away from her babies. Now this is her last baby, and she is again planning to return to work, but with each passing day she feels less and less inclined to return.

Still, she and her husband have come to depend on her salary. Beyond that, however, returning appeals to her because she loves her work. It is easy to see why she is successful: She is a ball of energy and charisma. In addition to these personal attributes, she has a well-defined professional philosophy: "I love helping people articulate and then deliver a clear and focused message."

Both in her work and in her personal life, I could see that she likes straight talk and detests wasting time. In sum, that is why she feels angry about going to the synagogue. She considers herself to be a spiritual person but finds that "almost none of my spirit is touched or fed by Jewish prayer or services. And usually, the rabbis just don't talk to me."

When we were finished speaking, she found a direct mail piece she had received and saved from an area church that offers "hip" pastors, relevant messages, great day care, cool music, and a casual atmosphere. Waving the piece, she said, "I've been tempted to go there, but I don't really want to. I love being Jewish; I just wish I could find something Jewish like this. In a way, this reminds me of the many wonderful Jewish experiences I had at Jewish summer camps. I miss that Jewish feeling and spirit we had at camp."

She said she's pretty much stopped going to services because "they are a waste of my time and I don't have time to waste." Still, she feels guilty and would like to find a place for her family. She and her husband joined a synagogue so they could enroll their kids in the nursery school. "The school was nurturing and wonderful, but — I know this is a bit of an exaggeration — still, it seems that synagogues only seem to know how to nourish people's souls if they are under the age of five."

Amy: There is a running joke in our family that when I was 10 years old, my parents made me start going to the synagogue. I came home after the first day and told my parents that I couldn't stand services. They said to me, "The day will come when you will thank us for making you go." Every year since then, and I'm now 43, after High Holiday services, I say to my parents, "I'm still waiting for the day to come."

Gil: *What's the problem?*

Amy: To me, the synagogue is a waste of time. The whole synagogue thing hardly ever works for me... which is the main reason I seldom go. You know, now I'm in "the house of God," boom, am I supposed to feel something?

Gil: *So what do you feel?*

Amy: Usually bored or frustrated.

Gil: *Because?*

Amy: There are a whole bunch of reasons. First, matters of God and spirituality are not something I can instantly get in touch with, just because I'm at a service. On top of that, I find prayer to be almost meaningless — I have a very hard time relating to that language. I also have mixed feelings about the rabbi. And as if that were not enough,

I feel like an incompetent klutz at the synagogue. Then, to add insult to injury, asking us to pay a huge amount of money in dues is offensive and wrong. Who do they think they are?

Gil: *Is that all?*

Amy: Isn't that enough?

Gil: *Yeah, I was just kidding. What would you say if I told you I share many of your frustrations?*

Amy: I thought you were a synagogue regular.

Gil: *Depends what you call a regular. I do often show up on a Saturday morning—purposely late. I usually come for less than an hour of the service. I seldom have patience for more than that. There are parts of being at the synagogue that I obviously like—such as seeing friends — or I wouldn't go. Still, I can relate to many of the things you*

> **"I've wondered what a Martian would think if he were plopped in the middle of a Jewish service. I think I know, because I feel like a Martian there."**

have said. It's very easy for me to see why people do not come to services. I have to work very hard to eke some meaning out of the service, and I have to say I often fail—and I'm trying. If I were less motivated, I think I'd always fail. So I find many of the reasons you mentioned fit for me. I take what you have to say seriously.

Amy: My reasons are very serious. I'd also say that I doubt I'm going to feel differently, even if we talk about these issues.

Gil: *That could be. Like I say, I've also had a difficult time struggling with some of the same issues and still do. I can't say that I have great answers for all these issues, but I've found answers to some of them, and for others I'm still looking. Through it all, though, I've concluded that the goal of Jewish worship and spirituality is to help us become better people. I like that goal. But I wouldn't care to force my answers on you. Matters of spirituality are quite personal.*

Amy: I appreciate that, but you don't have to worry about me. If the answers don't make sense to me, I'll tell you or I'll just ask you more questions. Still, I could use some answers because I'd like my children to be bar mitzvahed someday, and it would be nice to have those bar mitzvahs at a synagogue where I could find some warmth and spiritual fulfillment. To be honest, though, I'm not sure that's realistic. When it comes to synagogues, I just have so many issues.

Gil: *One thing you said is that "you feel like a klutz at the synagogue." What did you mean by that?*

Amy: I'd say that one big reason is the language. And don't tell me to try a temple where most of the service is in English. I have tried that and, even still, there is always some Hebrew. I read Hebrew like a preschooler and I pronounce it even worse. Plus, even in English the prayers are meaningless to me, and I really don't understand what's going on during the service… bowing and marching and Torah kissing, and on and on. I've wondered what a Martian would think if he were plopped in the middle of a Jewish service. I think I know, because I feel like a Martian there. Compare this to how I feel in my professional life, where I like to believe I'm a competent and capable person. Now are you surprised I don't enjoy the synagogue?

Gil: *No, I'm not surprised. What you said makes perfect sense to me. But how did you become competent at work?*

Amy: I went to college, and I learned a lot on the job — from colleagues and mostly by learning from mistakes. I see where you're going with this — but I think the prayer service is a lot different than my career. To start with, I don't conduct my work life in a foreign language that I don't understand.

Gil: *You're right about the language... which I have some thoughts on, that can wait. Still, I think the analogy fits — in fact, your career is probably more complicated than the service. I've found that the service is actually pretty simple and can be explained, believe it or not, in a matter of minutes. Figuring out what's going on is not rocket science... but you'll need to ask some questions. The logical person to ask is a rabbi. But you said you have mixed feelings about rabbis. What's that about?*

Amy: By and large, I think rabbis are good people who mean well. But in my personal and professional life, I care a lot about messages and how they are communicated. I have very little patience for a message I can't relate to, and I get particularly irritated when that message is communicated poorly. That's why, when it comes to rabbis, I often feel that we're not connecting.

Gil: *Are you saying you can't relate to rabbis' messages or to the way they communicate those messages?*

Amy: Both. Usually, that is. Though as a teenager, I was very impressed with our rabbi—he was always talking about the civil rights movement and the Vietnam war and a sense of right and wrong. And his delivery was so powerful and captivating. He truly inspired me. But that was an exception for me. Even though the rabbis I have met personally seem like sensitive and nice people, most of the rabbis I've heard over the years don't talk to me — though they certainly know how to talk and talk and talk.

Gil: *So do talk shows.*

Amy: That's true, but I would call that entertainment.

Gil: *Me, too, but I think most of us have gotten pretty used to being entertained by talk. And if it's not entertaining, we tune it out... unless, of course, it can be said in 20 seconds. Our expectations nowadays are pretty high.*

Amy: Wait a minute, no pun intended, are you trying to blame me for being bored by rabbis? Wouldn't you say that's blaming the victim?

Gil: *Yes and no. There is no question that some rabbis can speak and some can't. But you can find one that does speak to you... in a reasonable amount of time.*

Amy: That's a lot easier said than done. I find rabbis are unapproachable.

> **"It seems that many congregations look for their rabbi to become a chief operating officer instead of a teacher and spiritual leader."**

Gil: *I used to share that opinion with you, but now I don't think that it's fair to generalize about rabbis like that. I've found that an approachable rabbi is a matter of personality and chemistry. For example, I've met rabbis who like to be called Rabbi and I've met others who like to be called by their first name. Doctors are the same way. And many people prefer one choice over the other. You need to find someone whose personal style is compatible with yours.*

Amy: It's not just style. It seems that rabbis at synagogues are so busy "running" the place that they don't pay attention to the people.

Gil: *I've actually talked to several rabbis about that. I have yet to meet a rabbi whose "calling" to the rabbinate was because he or she wanted to become an administrator. It seems that many congregations look for their rabbi to become a chief operating officer instead of a teacher and spiritual leader.*

Amy: I will say it's hard to imagine an inspired young rabbinical student dreaming of someday doing his or her life work governed by a board of directors. Still, that's reality. Combine that with the style issue I mentioned before, I just don't think I could find a rabbi for me.

Gil: *I think you could if you wanted to, but it might take a little searching on your part.*

Amy: Okay, let's say I was willing to search for a rabbi for me. I still don't find that rabbis talk to me.

Gil: *Personally, I have found that to be true and not true.*

Amy: What do you mean?

Gil: *Well, most of the rabbis I have met seem to love answering questions. After all, the word "rabbi" means teacher. When I've asked rabbis questions about things that matter to me, I have found I can usually connect. Not only that, I've learned many things from rabbis that I believe have made me a better person. From the pulpit, unfortunately, I am often disappointed. Too often it seems to me that the rabbi is giving a sermon that would be great if the whole congregation was made up of other rabbis. That aggravates me. It's as if they're oblivious to the audience. The rabbis I can relate to speak in plain English about current events, the books, the movies, the business dilemmas, relationship questions, and other parts of life I have questions about — and what Judaism has to say about these issues.*

Amy: When rabbis speak about those issues, I do find value in their sermons. But more often than not, to me, the rabbis' comments seem out of touch with the way regular people lead their lives today. This discussion reminds me of a joke I heard about a farmer whose chickens were dying, so he went to the rabbi for advice. The rabbi told him to take away the water from his chickens for a few days. The farmer came back a few days later and said even more of his chickens had died. So the rabbi told him to give the water back to the chickens and take away their food for a few days. The farmer came back a few days later and said, "Rabbi, I've been following all of your advice and my chickens continue to die. Do you have any more advice?" And the rabbi said, "I have plenty more advice. Do you have any more chickens?" My point is that I'm not sure I'm really interested in what Moses or anyone else in the Bible or the rabbi has to say about my life.

Gil: *I can understand why you might say that, and that's a pretty good joke, too. On the other hand, I've spoken to people who have expressed similar sentiments but later in the conversation tell me they would be curious to hear what rabbis think on many subjects. For example, they would like to hear rabbis honestly speak about whether or not they believe in God — and then to define God.*

Amy: That would intrigue me.

Gil: *I don't think you would have a hard time coming up with a number of issues that would intrigue you.*

Amy: Well, I have wondered about what Judaism says about fetal research or, on the other end of the continuum, life after death or ethical business practices or single-parent adoptions — actually, a lot of things.

Gil: *Like I said, there is no shortage of issues. And I agree with you, finding a rabbi who can relate and talk to you is not easy. I think part of the solution is that we have to change our expectations.*

Amy: What do you mean?

Gil: *I mean that getting direction about a challenging issue may be difficult to do quickly. That does not mean I think rabbis need more than 20 minutes to address a topic or need to speak in language that only a professor or another rabbi can relate to. I personally can't stand that. But I don't expect 60-second explanations either. Learning and getting some spiritual satisfaction should be enjoyable, but it's not exactly like entertainment or instant results, like throwing a bag of popcorn in the microwave.*

Amy: All right. I can accept what you're saying — except speaking as a marketing and communications professional, I believe a message can and should be conveyed in 15 minutes or less. But as I told you, my problems with the synagogue go beyond the rabbi. I hardly ever get anything out of the prayer book or prayer, for that matter. It's not learning, it's not enjoyable, it's not entertainment, and the last thing it is for me is spiritual.

Gil: *You said "hardly ever." When have you gotten something out of the prayer book?*

Amy: Sometimes on the High Holidays, when I'm thinking about what I did during the year and how I could be a better person, I can feel moved by some of the prayers. But I'm in a different frame of mind at those times. I know the service is coming, and it just seems a lot more serious to me.

Gil: *It makes sense to me that you would find that a spiritual experience. Just as it made sense to me that you don't feel competent when you're at the service. I once heard a good explanation: opera and football.*

Amy: Excuse me, but you just lost me.

Gil: *If you were to take the average person off the street and make them sit in the front row of an Italian opera for two hours, what would that person get out of the opera?*

Amy: Probably a strong desire to hurt me — badly.

Gil: *Hopefully not, but they would not likely get very much out of what they experienced. Something like this did actually happen at a football game. The way I heard the story, President Nixon "treated" Secretary General Brezhnev of the ex-Soviet Union to an NFL football game. After the game, Brezhnev was asked at a press conference what he thought of the game. He responded, "All fall down, all get up. All fall down, all get up." That's all an unprepared person got out of America's most popular spectator sport.*

Amy: That's a cute story… sounds like my husband. He is always telling me that I'm missing an entire dimension of life because I have almost no interest or understanding of team sports. Now I suppose you're going to tell me that this is the same as prayer.

Gil: *Not exactly. The similarity is that football, opera, and prayer will be meaningless unless you prepare for what you're about to experience. Worse yet, they will probably bore you to tears. The good news is that the opposite can be true if you prepare. Like you say, they can offer you an entire dimension of life. But with prayer, it ain't easy. Personally, I find football is a lot easier.*

Amy: So maybe that's why the High Holiday service sometimes is meaningful for me.

Gil: *I think so. You said you were in the right frame of mind ahead of time. This may seem strange, but it sounds like you were kind of "psyched up" for a spiritual experience. You were ready to think about how you acted over the past year and how you might change in the coming year.*

> **"I hardly ever get anything out of the prayer book or prayer, for that matter. It's not learning, it's not enjoyable, it's not entertainment, and the last thing it is for me is spiritual."**

Amy: But that's only on the High Holidays — and only occasionally, at that. On a regular basis, this just doesn't work for me.

Gil: *Why?*

Amy: I'd say mostly because of the stiff language of the prayer book, and the whole God idea there I find difficult or impossible to believe.

Gil: *What's the "God idea" that you find so hard to believe?*

Amy: You know, God will hear my prayers and do things for me. This God of the prayer book who intercedes and performs miracles. I just don't buy it.

Gil: *I tend to agree with you. I have a different way of looking at prayer and God that I want to tell you about. But first I wanted to mention something a rabbi once pointed out to me. He told me I was wrong to talk about "a" God of the prayer book.*

Amy: What did he mean?

Gil: *He pointed out to me that there are more than 100 metaphors for God in the prayer book.*

Amy: One hundred? For example?

Gil: *If you're interested — or bored the next time you're at services — start paging through the prayer book. There's God the life force, the Creator of nature, the Provider, the Giver of wisdom, the Rock, Parent, Healer, Sustainer, Shepherd — you could go on and on.*

Amy: Even if I could find that in the language of the prayer book, that still sounds too much like a person or an object for me. I'm not sure these metaphors would do anything for me, because I just don't believe God is up there listening to prayers and answering.

> **"I wouldn't confidently say what God is or is not, does or doesn't do — because I just don't know... I have a hard time believing God is like a genie granting wishes."**

Gil: *There is obviously no way to prove one way or another what God is doing or not doing. But I'll tell you about something that happened to me.*

Amy: I hope you're not going to tell me that God came to you one night and personally spoke to you.

Gil: *No, it was during breakfast. Actually, what I was going to say is that my wife and I had twins who were born three months prematurely.*

Amy: Three months? Oh my God, how small were they?

Gil: *My daughter dropped to two pounds, but actually my son, who was nine ounces bigger, was in much more critical condition. Anyway, what I was going to say is that they were both on respirators and in bad shape in the intensive care unit of our local children's hospital. We were afraid to name them after relatives at first, because we thought the babies might die. A lot of Jewish and non-Jewish friends and even mere acquaintances told us that they were praying for us. And I have to say, though I admit this sounds like the Twilight Zone or something, I could almost tangibly feel all those people praying. I can't say what God heard or did, but it sure gave us strength, and I believe that it helped them get better.*

Amy: I could see how you gained strength, and how that helped your twins. But I have a very tough time believing God gained anything or intervened.

Gil: *I'm not sure I believe that either, though I heard a beautiful saying once that human beings are God's language. I would modify it a little to say that kind human actions are God's language.*

Amy: That's a nice thought.

Gil: *It moves me. Still, again I wouldn't confidently say what God is or is not, does or doesn't do — because I just don't know. As I said, I have a hard time believing God is like a genie granting wishes. I have a different notion of God and prayer.*

Amy: Yes?

Gil: *I think more in terms of finding help, direction, or strength from God, the silent partner.*

Amy: Don't you think that is just your conscience acting as a silent partner?

Gil: *Maybe. I have thought that. But then I've wondered, where does conscience come from? Then I made a discovery that further influenced my thinking about this: The Hebrew word "to pray" is correctly translated as "to judge or examine yourself."*

Amy: Are you suggesting that I think of prayer as self-examination or reflection time?

Gil: *If you want to. Personally, I usually find the silent meditation section of the service to be the most meaningful part for me. But as I said, how you feel about prayer and God is very personal. I wouldn't presume to tell you what is correct for you. You did say, though, that on the High Holidays, the self-examination approach seems to work for you.*

Amy: That's true, but that's once a year. On a regular basis, frankly, I'm not the type to get into "meditation" and self-examination.

Gil: *I didn't think I was either, but I've come to the realization that I probably do it more often than I thought. I wouldn't be surprised if you're the same way.*

Amy: What do you mean?

Gil: *To me, prayer is when I think about things bigger than me. A moment or more when I consciously marvel at something inspirational, or when I'm grateful for health or good fortune, or reflect on how to become better or to look for sources of strength beyond me to get over fear or discomfort. Prayer can take a lot of forms for me.*

Amy: If that's how you're defining prayer, then you're right, I think I already do that, probably not enough really. But I do marvel at things — like how much food comes out of my puny little garden, how my kids are growing, or how regular the tides are — all kinds of things, but I never considered any of these thoughts prayer. I've always thought of Jewish prayer as asking God to change things for us.

Gil: *I suspect some people pray that way. As for me, to paraphrase Kierkegaard, I'm far from confident that prayer makes God change the world, but I do think prayer can change people.*

> **"I don't think many adults pray for a new car. Like deep down, we know that doesn't seem right..."**

Amy: Like how?

Gil: *I think prayer helps people get in touch with what really matters in their heart of hearts. For example, even though most adults spend their daily life driven to accumulate money, I don't think many adults pray for a new car. Like deep down, we know that doesn't seem right, because a car doesn't really matter.*

Amy: I've heard jokes about praying to win the lottery.

Gil: *So have I, but we know they're jokes. Can you imagine actually getting on your knees and praying for your stocks to go up?*

Amy: There is something pathetic about that. No one has ever discussed prayer like this with me before. To get used to this would take some adjusting of my thinking. But I still don't think I need the synagogue to pray — especially if the point is self-reflection.

Gil: *You don't. Judaism says you can pray by yourself. But there is no question that Judaism finds value in praying in a group. For that matter, so do Christianity, Islam, Native American religions, and others. There can be something powerful and spiritual about praying together with others who are praying. Plus, I don't think self-reflection is the only goal—being connected to others and thinking about others is also a Jewish goal of prayer. On top of that, there is something to be said for structure.*

Amy: Structure? I don't think I like the sound of that.

Gil: *It does sound a little harsh. I think structure is one of the things people resent about organized religion. But in this case, I don't have a problem. I think Judaism realized that human nature is to take things for granted—that is, until we no longer have them. So to get us to appreciate what we have and to get in touch with our spirituality, structured into Jewish life are places to worship with others and a schedule of daily prayer services.*

Amy: So we will regularly examine our lives?

Gil: *That's the plan, at least. Judaism says if we do that daily—not just on the High Holidays—we will become better people. It's sort of like exercise—our daily spiritual workout. To be honest, even though I respect Jewish thinking on this subject, I've got to admit I'm not one to get into any kind of regular exercise routine—physical or spiritual. I feel better after I do it, but I'm seldom crazy about the idea.*

Amy: That makes two of us. And I certainly don't get anything out of going to a structured place of worship with a prayer book to get my "spiritual exercise." I don't mean to sound like I'm not interested in becoming a better person. There are times I really do appreciate a session of self-examination. I think the Jewish ideal is admirable, but if I were to "force" myself to pray daily, especially with a prayer book, the only exercise I think I'd get would be in frustration.

Gil: *I know what you mean. Still, I've found a prayer that almost always works—even if you don't believe in God.*

Amy: Sounds good...

Gil: *I'm talking about prayer that focuses on what we already have. I can do this with or without a prayer book.*

Amy: What do you mean?

Gil: *Like lying in bed at night before I go to sleep, I like to do sort of a quick inventory of the big things in life that I feel grateful to have, like health, my kids, and my family. Like I said, I don't know if my feeling thankful does anything for God, but I do think it helps me be a better person. It helps me appreciate "having," and those who do not have.*

> **"I've found a prayer that almost always works — even if you don't believe in God."**

Amy: That sounds fine to me. I think I do that, too, from time to time, but how do you do that with a prayer book? Those words seem so meaningless.

Gil: *For me, that's a lot harder — but it can be done.*

Amy: Why bother? I mean, why should I invest all the time and effort to find meaning in the prayer book?

Gil: *That's a tough question. I think part of the answer is that there is value in a prepared script, even if you're planning to ad lib. I think you can also find guidance in the prayer book by seeing what have been priorities for our people over the ages when they searched for spirituality. I think one of the easiest places to see this is in the blessings. They don't ask God anything. They express wonder and thanks. The morning blessings are good examples. They talk about things like the morning sun, how our bodies work, and so on. In Hebrew these prayers are called the* Bircote Hashachar.

Amy: Hold it. Before we talk any more about the prayer book, I want to talk about the language issue already. I told you how I feel about

Hebrew. I don't know Hebrew. I can barely read Hebrew. No parlez vous Hebrew. Comprende?

Gil: *I get it, and I have three suggestions. The first one you probably won't be wild about. Unfortunately, there is no way to learn another language without work. The work can be enjoyable or it can be a drag, depending on how motivated you are and how good you are at it.*

Amy: Well, I'm not good at it and I'm not very motivated. So give me the second suggestion.

Gil: *Okay. This one may be a bit of a stretch and may sound a little bizarre, but for some people there can actually be something spiritual about hearing but not understanding the "holy" language. You sort of let yourself mentally drift. Like have you ever heard a Latin mass?*

Amy: You don't need to mention Latin. My Hebrew is on par with my Latin. I see your point, and sometimes there can be something lofty or inspiring about not understanding the singing. But in general, my reaction is that it doesn't work for me.

Gil: *I thought you might say that. In that case, my third suggestion is English.*

Amy: I have a one-word response to the English of the prayer book — ugh!

Gil: *Could you be a little more specific?*

Amy: I suppose "ugh" isn't very eloquent, is it? What I mean is that I find the English of the prayer book formal and dull; it just doesn't talk to me. It sounds like something the Queen of England might say.

Gil: *I'm pretty sure the Queen of England does not get a lot out of a*

> **"Even when I'm trying hard to find meaning in many of the prayers, I'm usually put off by the translations."**

Jewish prayer book either, and to tell you the truth, most of the time, neither do I. I agree with you that the translation can be tough to relate to. Even when I'm trying hard to find meaning in many of the prayers, I'm usually put off by the translations.

Amy: Well, we agree on that one. So why did you suggest English?

Gil: *Because I suggest using English differently. I didn't get anything out of the English until I stopped looking at the exact literal meaning of the words and started using a little imagination.*

Amy: Imagination?

Gil: *A rabbi once told me that I should not be literal on purpose. He told me that if I want to pick the words apart, I should go to a class on prayer. He felt that a rational "thinking" approach to prayer defeats the purpose. The purpose, he told me, is to get you in touch with your soul, not your brain—to get you into a "prayerful mood," as he put it.*

Amy: I suppose if I were in the right frame of mind, that might work for me. But as a rule, the mentally drifting approaches are just not for me.

Gil: *Okay, then you might like a different approach to the English that I sometimes use — my own personal translation. Again, it involves not taking every word so literally.*

Amy: Like what?

Gil: *Well, to use the blessings as an example, most blessings start with the words: "Blessed are You Lord our God, King of the Universe—* Baruch Atah Adonai Eloheinu Melech ha olam."

Amy: Hey, I know those words. They were the only six words I learned to read in Hebrew school. But that's exactly what I mean. This is the kind of language that turns me off.

Gil: *Okay, try this instead. The blessing over eating bread, the famous* motzee, *is formally translated as: "Blessed are You Lord our God,*

King of the Universe, who extracts bread from the earth." If you want, you can translate it like this: "I'm in awe of a force greater than me. Dirt becomes flour and we have food. I'm grateful."

Amy: I'm sorry to be so negative, but that sounds a little too "touchy-feely" for me.

Gil: You can use any words you want, whatever fits for you: God, awesome, wonder, miracle… The point is, you can translate prayers into whatever language is meaningful to you.

Amy: In theory, these suggestions are all fine. At a minimum, they are thought-provoking. I just have a difficult time thinking of myself actually doing much of this.

Gil: You might not. I must say that by myself and at the synagogue, I'm often not moved to pray or by prayer. So I can easily understand why you say this is difficult. Hopefully, what we have talked about can help a little. Minimally, you should be less bored the next time you're at services.

Amy: I'll accept the possibility that these suggestions could offer me something — except for one thing.

Gil: Synagogue dues.

Amy: How did you know?

Gil: Because I didn't forget you said that at the outset. But I purposely waited until now to mention dues, since you said you were getting little or nothing out of a synagogue membership. I figured, what's the use of talking about the cost if you don't find spirituality or anything else at the synagogue that you perceive has value?

> **"I really feel repulsed by the emphasis on dollars and fundraising at the synagogue."**

Amy: That's kind of weird, because even before this conversation, I did occasionally enjoy or find something worthwhile for me at the synagogue—but not much. I think I could find even more value now if I tried. But I'm not sure it's worth trying. I really feel repulsed by the emphasis on dollars and fundraising at the synagogue.

Gil: *I only know one answer to that issue: Try to find a place where you find comfort and value. The sad reality of life is that everything is expensive—including offering religious services, running buildings, nursery and religious schools, other programs, and paying salaries.*

Amy: If I was regularly taking advantage of these things, I might feel comfortable paying for them. But I don't.

Gil: *I suspect a lot of people feel that way. As a rule, I have found that people don't mind paying high dollars if they feel they're getting their money's worth... sometimes even if they don't get their money's worth, like some of the clubs people join. As for synagogues, most of the time, most congregants don't use the many costly services provided — that is, until their baby is born, or it's time for nursery school or a bar mitzvah, or marriage comes up, or there is a family emergency, sickness, or death — then they expect the rabbi to be on call for them and the facilities to be available. Whether a person uses those things or not, having them on standby and meeting those kinds of demands costs a lot of money.*

Amy: But that doesn't mean people have a right to demand that I pay a certain amount of money or I cannot participate at the synagogue.

Gil: *You realize, of course, that none of that money ends up in their pockets. The people who have the unpleasant task of managing a synagogue budget are usually volunteers, and their job wins them few friends. Most nonprofits—and synagogues are no exception—are always scrambling to make ends meet. So the volunteers on the budget committee are usually given the responsibility of deciding what a person's "fair share" should be. Some synagogues just have set rates. But often dues are based on income—those who can least afford to pay are asked to pay less, and vice versa. Either way, the result is often that someone takes offense… especially when that person chooses to hardly ever use the synagogue.*

Amy: That would include me, and while we're on the subject of money, I have to mention another source of discomfort. I am just disgusted by the emphasis on expensive cars, furs, jewelry, designer clothing, and lavish bar mitzvahs that synagogues and temples seem to have. All of this detracts from spirituality for me.

Gil: *This is a major turnoff for me, too. I've found a simple solution. I choose not to keep up with the Joneses — or should I say Cohens. I wouldn't belong to that kind of synagogue.*

Amy: That is easier said than done.

Gil: *Maybe. But it can be done. If issues of dues, materialism, or whatever are a problem for you, then again I'd say to find a place where you do feel comfortable. A big part of the comfort includes a place where you find meaning. One place you might want to explore would be a* havurah. *They are small groups that get together for a service — often for a meal and socializing too. There are hundreds of them around the country. They even have a national organization you can call that will hook you up with a* havurah *near you.*

Amy: That sounds interesting — do they charge dues?

Gil: *Some do, some don't. Some include kids, some don't. Some are part of a temple or synagogue, and some are informally organized with no building or rabbi. If the synagogue is not for you, check out an independent* havurah.

Amy: I must confess, you have made some discoveries about synagogue and prayer that are new to me — though you have not erased all of my concerns.

Gil: *Oh, I didn't think I would — especially since I haven't erased all of my own concerns yet, either.*

Amy: I would love to see a synagogue, temple, or rabbi ask me some of the questions you asked me. If they were really interested in the needs of Jews, then they should ask us, listen to us, and be prepared to make changes.

Key Points to Hold Onto

Chapter 4: "There's No Spirituality for Me in Synagogues and Prayer"

- Finding a rabbi you can relate to could take some searching.

- The service will probably not be meaningful unless:

  1. you feel competent — this is easier to do than you may suspect,

  2. you are in the right frame of mind,

  3. you can relate to the images of God in the prayer book (there are over 100).

- There are a number of ways to look at prayer beyond asking God to intervene:

  1. think in terms of "judging or examining yourself" — that is what the Hebrew word "to pray" means literally,

  2. take a look at Jewish blessings; they are prayers of awe and thanks,

  3. you do not have to be bound to the words of the prayer book to pray.

- If issues of dues, money, and materialism offend you, check out a different synagogue, temple, or *havurah*.

Afterthoughts

After reading this book, one person wrote to tell me that for worship to be spiritually uplifting for him, it had to be uniquely personal. He objected to rote reading, and for him, the prescribed format of the Jewish worship detracted from personal spirituality. This may sound strange, but his comment reminded me of a Billy Joel concert I once attended. The concert culminated with Billy Joel's classic hit "Piano Man." He led the entire audience (it felt more like a congregation) in singing the refrain: "Sing us a song, you're the piano man. Sing us a song tonight. Well, we're all in the mood for a melody, and you've got us feelin' alright. La la la…" We sang with gusto and the collective strength of almost 15,000 souls. There was something wonderful about this powerful singing in unison, and yet I think each one of us experienced the joy of the moment in our own uniquely personal way.

I had a similar though less dramatic experience during a sermon I once heard given by an expert in Jewish liturgical music. As part of his sermon, he too led the congregation in the unison singing of a short section of a prayer. When we had finished, he told us that as he listened to us, he heard a collective power in our voices, yet he saw on each face a different expression. His point, I believe, was to show us that worshipping collectively can create a power and spirituality that can touch each person and enhance their individual prayer. While saying this, I can still understand the sentiment of the person who contacted me — especially since he told me that he did not understand Hebrew or the logic behind any of the service.

Some who read this chapter told me that I was too apologetic for rabbis, synagogues, temples, and all that goes on there. Others who read this chapter acknowledged their responsibility for some of the problems they experienced in services. My response to all of these thoughts is that being defensive was certainly not my intention, nor was pointing fingers. I've tried to be fair.

My purpose in this chapter was to air the issues I have heard and to offer some thoughts that might help you find some value in Jewish worship. After all is said and done, I have concluded that when it comes to reaching people spiritually, many things we Jews do are right and much needs to change.

I believe there is great wisdom and value in our spiritual infrastructure — our liturgy, our places of worship, and our religious leadership. At the same time, I also believe that unless all three undergo significant change, more and more Jews will avoid what Judaism has to offer spiritually — and I can't say I blame them. As I mentioned in the chapter, far too often, I have also felt frustrated and unfulfilled by services.

Specifically, what are some of those changes, and what are we doing right, you may ask? That could probably fill a book by itself. In a few words, in the change department, if it were up to me, I would eliminate as much formality as possible; I would personalize more of the service. I would change prayers to everyday language. I would shorten sermons and the entire service for that matter. I would increase interaction during the service between the pulpit and the congregation. I would get rid of robes. I would use singing and music differently. I would experiment. And I could go on.

On the positive side, to me the idea that Jews do not need an intermediary to be spiritual is important and meaningful. I also like the idea of silent meditation as a part of all services. In addition, I appreciate the participation of children and the relatively lenient attitude about visiting with neighbors that I have experienced in many services. And I could go on.

In this book, however, I won't. I hope substantive changes will occur soon, but today, even without these changes, I can find benefit through contact with rabbis, prayer, synagogues, and temples. I hope this chapter offered you some ideas that can assist you in finding some benefit as well.

Questions From This Chapter You May Wish to Ponder

- Have you had a meaningful Jewish spiritual experience?

- How did it happen? Or what was spiritual about it?

- If a rabbi gave you carte blanche to change the synagogue or temple, what changes would you make?

Chapter 5
"I Have a Love-Hate Relationship With the Jewish Community"

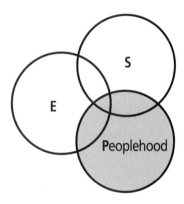

From what I heard, I concluded that the peoplehood circle is the easiest and most tangible way for most people to feel Jewish. As this chapter shows, there are many ways this can happen. For example, imagine how you would feel in the following situation — which happened to me. My wife and I were with three other Jewish couples at a comedy act when the comedian asked if there were any Jews in the audience. We were the only ones to raise our hands in the packed house. He then proceeded to tell a couple of Jewish jokes that were borderline anti-Semitic.

Later, we were speaking among ourselves and we all agreed that we felt the same sense of uneasiness as we waited for the punch lines — and afterward. These feelings that we all shared are part of peoplehood or belonging to the Jewish people.

If you felt similarly as you read about that incident or have felt proud as a Jew to read of an accomplishment of a fellow Jew, then you were identifying with the Jewish people and are in the peoplehood circle.

Many aspects of experiencing the Jewish way of life in the peoplehood circle are wonderful — like a sense of belonging. Other aspects are difficult and unpleasant. This chapter probes the complexities and contradictory feelings that come with belonging to the Jewish people.

Rick

"I'm one of those guys that I guess everybody is writing about: I will probably intermarry," Rick volunteered matter-of-factly to start our discussion. "And I should say from the outset that even though my girlfriend is Lutheran, I don't find that to be an issue, nor does it affect my being Jewish —which I'm proud to be."

Rick, who is 28, met his girlfriend Kathy through work three years ago. Rick works in his family's business, a hospital supply company, and met Kathy when he was making a sales call at the hospital where she was a nurse. He stopped her to ask for directions and was smitten. Those directions, Rick suspects, will ultimately lead all the way to an altar soon. Though not a synagogue's altar, which is a source of bitterness for Rick.

"From what I understand, I will have a hard time finding a rabbi to co-officiate at our wedding, even though Kathy says finding a minister would be no problem. I know my parents would die if I ever got married in a church, so we'll probably end up using a judge."

This is frustrating to Rick for two reasons. First, he thinks that kind of attitude from the Jewish community only repels Jews like himself and is counterproductive. Second, he does not understand why his parents suddenly care so much about Judaism, since when he was growing up, they did very little in their home or life to encourage Judaism. For example, they belonged to a synagogue but only went on the High Holidays. "I think my parents are hypocrites to make such a big deal of my marrying a non-Jew. Especially since my parents have come to see that Kathy is a wonderful person and that she and I really love each other. In fact, over time they have become very fond of her.

"Kathy's family always accepted me. My religion to them is not an issue. She and her family seem to view Judaism with great respect. I'm embarrassed that the feelings from my family have not always been mutual." In spite of this, "to her great credit," Rick says that Kathy is prepared to make a commitment to Rick to raise their children as Jews.

This and every other aspect of Rick's Judaism are a puzzle to Kathy. "We share so many interests," he said, "reading, the outdoors, sports, music, just about everything. But she just can't understand what being Jewish means to me, since I don't actively practice anything especially Jewish. To tell the truth, I think Kathy is right to be confused, since I can't really explain to her, or to myself, for that matter, why I care so much about having myself and my future children belong to the Jewish people."

Rick: My family gave me a lot of grief over Kathy. I mean, here I was in love with a bright, beautiful, kind, and caring person, and my family felt they had a right to reject her just because she was not Jewish.

Gil: *Sounds awful…*

Rick: That's an understatement. They made my life miserable for a long time. I considered breaking off contact with them altogether, but after all, they are my family—the only family I have. Deep down I always knew that they really cared about me. And of course, I care about them too. It's taken time, but thankfully they have come around. What really irritates me now is that it seems like the whole Jewish community is still on my case.

Gil: *How so?*

Rick: I sense a pressure from the Jewish community that I really resent. Like trying to find a rabbi who might marry us. I especially can't stand the "cliquishness" and guilt of the Jewish community—not just about Kathy but about everything I do.

Gil: *Like what?*

Rick: It's kind of hard for me to describe. I'd call it "community think." It's a pressure to act a certain way—like who I should marry, who I should give my money to, where I should live, what I should or shouldn't do. You know, God forbid anyone should see you do this or that. Like I received pressure because I didn't go to college—I sensed the expectation that "all Jews should go to college." The Jewish community just feels so meddlesome and "clannish."

Gil: *I can see how that would irritate you.*

Rick: Doesn't it irritate you?

Gil: *Sort of, but not so much anymore.*

Rick: Why not? What changed?

Gil: *Me. Visiting Israel helped me a lot. It helped give me a broader perspective of our people. I look at our community differently now. Instead of viewing it as clannish or cliquish, which is so negative, I have a more positive image. I think of the Jewish community as family. As you know all too well, families can be a pain, but in general, I wouldn't want to give mine up. I need the roots, and I like the feeling of belonging.*

Rick: Truth be told, in spite of my recent hassle with my family over Kathy, during my lifetime my family has probably been the best part of being Jewish to me. Maybe this is why I want my kids to be Jewish. I'm not sure. I do know that as I get older, I appreciate my family more and more.

Gil: *What is it you appreciate?*

Rick: We just have a lot in common that we don't need to explain to each other. That's why when we're together, there is a warm feeling, usually that is — especially during holiday get-togethers. I really look forward to them. That's not to say that we don't sometimes drive each other crazy.

Gil: *In a nutshell, that is how I now look at the Jewish community. Sometimes it can drive me crazy, but in general, I like the feeling that I have a lot in common with other Jews, just because we're Jewish.*

> **"I think of the Jewish community as family… families can be a pain, but in general, I wouldn't want to give mine up. I need the roots, and I like the feeling of belonging."**

Rick: I think I understand that. I'll give you kind of a funny example. After high school, I moved out of town and my mother kept nudging me to find a synagogue for the High Holidays. That's exactly the kind of thing I would normally ignore from my mom. I mean, I never go at home. But here I am 2,000 miles from home, and for some reason I listened to my mother and went. While I was there, I met another person who looked as lost as me. Turns out he was also from out of town. So I said, "Do you normally go to services?" He said, "Nope." So I said, "Neither do I, let's get out of here." And to this day he is one of my closest friends.

Gil: *Isn't that typical? That story just sounds Jewish. It seems complaining or kvetching to each other is Jewish. It's ironic that in this case what brought you together as Jews is that you both didn't want to be at the synagogue.*

Rick: I never quite thought of it in those terms, but I guess you're right. The way you put it, though, doesn't sound so great. I can remember a different example that sounds a little better. I once got invited to an Orthodox bar mitzvah, and I must say that place was great. Now that I mention it, I can't believe I liked an Orthodox synagogue.

Gil: *What was so great about it?*

Rick: What was great was the feeling. It's hard to describe, but it just seemed like a tight family — even though the men and women sat separately. Even I, Mr. Nonpracticing Jew, felt welcome. Someone actually came up to me during the service, introduced himself, and invited me over for a Sabbath lunch. It was amazing.

Gil: *You realize you used the word family?*

Rick: It really did seem like family. The kids were all running around and playing. The grown-ups didn't seem to care, they just gave the kids candy — even the rabbi did. In a strange way, even though the kids were disrupting the praying, it seems like they were somehow enhancing the service. The people there were really great — they made that place really alive. I've never really experienced anything like that before or since.

Gil: *So you no longer connect with Jewish people at the synagogue?*

Rick: Well, actually that's not exactly true. The one thing they do right at synagogue is the food after services — the *oneg* or *kiddish*, or whatever they call it. When I have to go to services, I console myself by stuffing myself with some pretty good home-made snacks and shmoozing. I do have to admit, the gathering and talking with people is usually quite enjoyable.

Gil: *For me too. In fact, it is one of the main reasons I go. I used to think that this was a substandard reason — but now I don't. In fact, did you know that the Hebrew word for synagogue,* bet ha-knesset, *does not mean house of worship? It means house of assembly.*

Rick: Is that why the parliament in Israel is called the Knesset?

Gil: *That's why. They gather together to make laws. But the point of the synagogue is to gather Jews together to create a sense of community.*

Rick: Are you telling me that synagogues are not built for prayer?

Gil: *Prayer is certainly one of the main reasons for gathering in a syna-gogue — but you can pray by yourself. You don't need a synagogue. But Judaism says we do need our people or community. Judaism even considers the community to be sacred. So the synagogue or temple is a place to gather the members of the Jewish community or people... not just for prayers, but to celebrate good times and give each other support in bad times. We gather together for meetings, weddings, funerals, parties, eating, talking, and socializing with each other.*

Rick: I never really thought of eating herring and shmoozing as sacred.

Gil: *In and of itself, I'd say calling that sacred is probably pushing it. But do you think it's a coincidence that eating and shmoozing after services is almost a religious ritual at virtu-ally every synagogue and temple? I believe it's a part of the high value Judaism places on community.*

> **"Judaism says we do need our people or community. Judaism even considers the community to be sacred."**

Rick: Don't you think that it's just because we Jews like to eat? I'm still not sure I get what you mean when you say the community is sacred.

Gil: *Maybe it will be more clear if I say "the Jewish people" or our "peoplehood." I think Judaism says that our peoplehood is sacred because it's bigger than each of us. As I mentioned, I feel this very strongly when I visit Israel. Kind of a cosmic way to put it is that each of us is a part of the Jewish people and the Jewish people is a part of each of us.*

Rick: I'm still not sure I understand.

Gil: *How about if I said every person needs a community and a community needs every person to make the community?*

Rick: Fine, but then why do I need the Jewish community?

Gil: *You don't. But it's yours, and that means a lot—at least it does to me. It seems to me that belonging is a basic human need. That's one reason why I think lost teenagers join gangs. As for me, I like the feeling of belonging to the Jewish people.*

Rick: Don't you think a basic human need is to be an individual?

Gil: *Yes, I think that's also a basic human need. But I haven't met many people who care to be so unique that they want to be nerds—to stand out awkwardly from the group or society they live with or to be isolated. Personally, I'm proud of who I am as an individual, and at the same time I love the feeling of belonging to the Jewish community and having the sense that I'm part of something bigger—the chain of our history and tradition.*

> **"When my grandfather suddenly passed away, I was devastated...
> I didn't feel I wanted God, the rabbi, or anyone spiritual. I needed my family, my friends, my community."**

Rick: Maybe that is why I want my kids to be Jewish. I want them to be individuals for sure, but I guess I'd also like them to belong and to be a part of the chain. At least, I don't want to be the one to break the chain.

Gil: *That's one reason I want my kids to be Jewish—not the only reason, but a good one.*

Rick: Being a part of a chain does fit for me, though I never quite thought of it in terms of "peoplehood." But it does make sense, and you're right, it does feel bigger than me.

Gil: *Ultimately, this is why I think Judaism says our "peoplehood" is sacred. I can often find something spiritual about this. Like I've been in synagogues in other cities where I have not liked the worshipping. But I did get something out of being together with my "people," even though the Jews there were total strangers to me.*

Rick: You just said something that clicked for me. When my grandfather suddenly passed away, I was devastated. He started our family's business. At the time, I didn't feel I wanted God, the rabbi, or anyone spiritual. I needed my family, my friends, my community. We sat shiva at my parents' home, and I didn't even know many of the people there, and I definitely didn't understand the service. But still I felt that I was surrounded by my people. It was important and comforting to me, and it was spiritual.

Gil: *Why? What happened? Was it what people said to you?*

Rick: No, it was what was not said. There was kind of an unspoken understanding and support. I just felt that we had a lot in common. There was a sensitivity in the air that was warm and comforting, and I can't exactly explain this, but it felt Jewish. I felt the people there were connected to me. I was with "my" people. I belonged to them and they belonged to me. Like I say, it was spiritual. It was good for my soul.

Gil: *That connected feeling is one of the things I like most about being Jewish. As you put it, we have sort of an unspoken shared understanding.*

Rick: We should, really. I mean, we have a lot in common. We have a shared past, shared values, we share the same Yiddish swear words, it even seems we share the same taste in food, like an aversion to white bread.

Gil: *I like white bread.*

Rick: Go figure.

Gil: *I told you I'm an individual. What you said brings up something else we Jews share: the feeling that we're different, that we're outsiders. Anti-Semitism is the extreme of this, but you can feel this outsider feeling in other ways — especially at Christmastime.*

Rick: That was especially hard for me when I was a kid. Santa was everywhere, and the Christmas lights and music and television shows — we get kind of bombarded. I feel much more comfortable now, especially since Kathy's family has shown me Christmas in a very positive and beautiful way. Still, I don't want my children to feel like outsiders the way I have in my life. I guess I'd like to find the best of both worlds.

Gil: *Like being an outsider and insider at the same time. They both have their advantages and disadvantages.*

Rick: That's what I mean. I'll give you another example that I know is going to sound paranoid. Before I went to work at my family's business, I worked at another company. It was a great place — I really enjoyed working there. The people there were a diverse, bright, capable, and nice group — they were wonderful, except for one thing. There was one other Jewish guy who worked there. It seemed like half the time my colleagues came up to me and called me Stuart — that was his name. And in my mind, I assumed they were thinking "Good morning, Jew, I mean Stuart, I mean…" I may be making this up in my head because I don't think they were anti-Semitic, but I just felt different.

Gil: *Do you think Stuart felt like you did?*

Rick: I'm pretty sure he did. We never spoke specifically about it, but I could just tell. It seems like, as Jews, we share kind of a quiet pain and anxiety — that in a way, I've got to say, I kind of like.

Gil: *You like the feeling?*

Rick: What I mean is that I have this feeling that there is something different between me and non-Jews. It's odd, because I find I truly enjoy and appreciate my non-Jewish friends and share many interests and values with them. And I've even fallen in love with a non-Jew, and her family is fantastic — I love them as well. Yet I sometimes feel like an outsider, like I can't exactly connect completely. There's something uncomfortable about it, but at the same time I kind of like feeling different.

> **"[Christmas] was especially hard for me when I was a kid. Santa was everywhere, and the Christmas lights and music and television shows — we get kind of bombarded."**

I feel a little unique. There is something special, something appropriate about it, and it seems that other Jews like Stuart share and understand this feeling with me.

Gil: *It really is being an outsider and an insider at the same time. Maybe we are getting some of the best of both worlds.*

Rick: Maybe we are. I've never really thought of this outsider/insider idea before. It also explains something I could never quite understand that I told you about earlier. When I travel for work, or if I'm at a party, I often find that I somehow eventually gravitate to the only Jewish person in the room. Gravitate is a good word, too — it's almost like a gravity force that seems to pull me. I'm not sure how it happens.

Gil: *What happens?*

Rick: It's really strange too. Because often when I'm around other Jews, I feel some kind of affinity there — even though, as I've said, I don't consider myself to be an "active" Jew. I have tried to explain this to Kathy and I can't. And as close as we are, she can't understand what I'm talking about and I've never been able to explain it.

Gil: *I've found an explanation that works. I describe it as meeting members of my extended family — or as a friend of mine always used to say, an "M.O.T." — a member of the tribe. Tribe, after all, does mean extended family. It's "peoplehood." It's like finding someone from your home town when you're out of town. You have a lot in common with each other — even though you're each obviously different. Being with other Jews is like being with family members. There is a lot we don't have to explain to each other — we just sort of know.*

Rick: That would also explain why I feel proud or embarrassed when I hear of a Jew who has done something great or terrible in the news.

Gil: *I think so. To me, they are like family — whether I like it or not. You know, there is another thing like family that happens among us Jews; we feel comfortable saying things to each other that we would never say to or ask of a stranger.*

Rick: I know what you mean, and that's one of the things that really bugs me. Just because I'm Jewish, I don't feel another Jew has the right to ask me to give money to this or that Jewish cause. I don't have an obligation to live my life any set way. I may be a member of the Jewish people, but like you said, I'm still an individual.

Gil: *In my life, there have been times when I have felt offended and resisted this "Jewish pressure" you're talking about. As I've gotten older, I've mellowed out. For one thing, I now realize that every group that we belong to exerts some pressure and obligations — just ask any teenager. The group they hang out with puts pressure on them about everything, what to wear, what to say and how to say it, whether to smoke or not, whether to have sex or not.*

Rick: I guess that pressure is the price kids pay for the benefit of belonging. But when it comes to being Jewish, I'm not a teenager and I don't care to put up with Jewish communal pressure.

Gil: *As I've gotten older, I've come to understand Jewish communal pressure better. I certainly don't always like it, but I realize it's a price I pay for the benefit of belonging. Today, broadly speaking, I think of it with more respect than contempt.*

Rick: I've also tried to understand it, but I've come to a different conclusion. I've concluded we're so community-minded because of persecution. I can accept that. But I don't think that's a good enough reason to continue to act and think so collectively.

Gil: *I think that persecution over the centuries is one of the reasons we Jews tend to think collectively. But I believe there is another, bigger reason. I've come to learn that compared to Western law, Jewish law and tradition is much more community oriented. I think this is a problem for so many Jews today because we're a product of a democratic legal system that places a high value on individual freedom.*

"It's really strange… often when I'm around other Jews, I feel some kind of affinity there — even though… I don't consider myself to be an 'active' Jew."

Rick: Is there something wrong with individual freedom?

Gil: *Not necessarily, but it clashes with a lot of classic Jewish thinking and law, since Jewish thinking places the well-being of the community over that of the individual.*

Rick: How can Judaism do that? I always thought Judaism cared so much about people.

Gil: *It only sounds like a contradiction — it isn't. It's just a different approach. Judaism places a high value on the uniqueness and importance of every human life. But according to Jewish thinking, we show our caring for individuals by having a healthy community. If the community is being well cared for, all the individuals in the community benefit. That doesn't sit right for most of us because we have been raised in a system that says the rights of the individual are so important.*

Rick: If you're telling me to choose between individual rights as offered by America or communal obligations as dictated by Judaism, I choose individual rights.

Gil: *So do most people, and so do I a lot of the time. But at the same time, as I said, I've come to respect the Jewish point of view. I think the community is often well served by collective obligations. For example, imagine what would happen if we let individual rights govern drinking and driving. And you don't have to imagine what would happen in the U.S. if individual rights governed whether you could own a gun or not. People certainly argue whether or not the community is well served by individuals having the right to own guns.*

> **"If you're telling me to choose between individual rights as offered by America or communal obligations as dictated by Judaism, I choose individual rights."**

Rick: Really, there are quite a few examples like that. Just open the newspaper. I often wonder if having so many individual rights has helped or hurt America.

Gil: *I've concluded both. There are up sides and down sides to having so many individual rights. For me, it is similar to my saying I can resent and respect the communal obligation of Judaism. In the case of*

Judaism, I've concluded that if obligation to my community is a price I have to pay to be part of the Jewish people, I think it's worth it.

Rick: But aren't you offended when you're asked to give money to a Jewish cause—just because you're Jewish?

Gil: *I'm not offended when Uncle Sam asks for my taxes. I may not be excited about it, but I appreciate it's a price I pay for the many wonderful benefits of being part of the American community. The same is true when Sam Goldstein calls me for a Jewish cause. I may not like his style or his choice of words, but I appreciate that he is asking on behalf of the Jewish community — my people, who would be here for me if I needed help. I'm not offended because I also feel I benefit by being part of the Jewish people. I get a feeling of belonging — to something wonderful.*

Rick: It goes beyond feelings. I have a friend who was born Jewish but has never practiced any aspect of being Jewish. His entire life he has had no attachment at all to Judaism or the Jewish community. His parents had zero interest in anything Jewish either—and they gave next to nothing to Jewish charities. But recently he needed all kinds of help with his mom, who is now a widow and has Alzheimer's. He called a local Jewish organization that works with the elderly and they were there in a flash, just because he and his mom are Jewish. I was amazed but somehow not surprised.

Gil: *Being part of the Jewish people has got its disadvantages, but I wouldn't care to trade. I love my Jewish roots and my extended family."*

Rick: Having roots and belonging really is worth a lot. I may always resent communal pressure and obligations, but I can see your point about the price of belonging and receiving benefits. At the same time, I think the Jewish community is going to have to change the way it treats Jews who fall in love with and marry non-Jews. Otherwise I'm not sure I—and, for sure, my future children—will be able to say that we're glad our roots and sense of belonging are with the Jewish people.

Key Points to Hold Onto

Chapter 5: "I Have a Love-Hate Relationship
With the Jewish Community"

- The Jewish community is similar to extended family. Like any family, belonging has its advantages and disadvantages.

- Jewish "peoplehood" is considered sacred.

- Feeling connected to other Jews is often unspoken and difficult to explain. Some of this feeling is pleasant, some is not.

- One of the conditions of being Jewish is a simultaneous feeling of being an outsider and an insider.

- There is a tension between the Western emphasis on the rights of the individual and the Jewish emphasis on obligations to the community.

- Being part of the Jewish people includes obligations and benefits.

Afterthoughts

A good example of the difference between the Western emphasis on the individual and the Jewish emphasis on peoplehood was described to me by Rabbi Michael Goldberg (who in the 1980s first started writing about the idea of Jewish master stories that is described in the next chapter). He said you can easily see this different emphasis by looking at national holidays.

Many American holidays celebrate individuals, (like Columbus Day, Presidents' Day, and Martin Luther King Day), but you will find no such holidays in Judaism. Although we certainly have had our heros, like Abraham, Moses, King David, and many modern individuals, most of our holidays celebrate events that happen to us as a people, such as Passover, Purim, and Hanukkah. This, he explained, is because our tradition and holidays seek to always remind us of the importance of our peoplehood.

This thinking has continued to our time. For example, today you will commonly see the United Jewish Communities (formerly the United Jewish Appeal, or UJA) and other Jewish organizations using slogans like "We are One," "One Destiny," and so on. I believe there are two reasons for this. First is because peoplehood is an important part of Judaism. The second reason is that these organizations recognize that many Jews easily place themselves in the peoplehood circle.

One nonreligious Jew who is quite active in the Jewish community told me that this chapter was helpful to him in this regard. The idea of peoplehood shed new light on his definition of who he was as a Jew.

I saw this same reaction on a large scale in 1992 and 1993 when I had two experiences that profoundly shaped my understanding of peoplehood. In those two years, I helped lead two experimental and hugely successful missions to Israel. The experiment, conducted by the Minneapolis Federation for Jewish Service, was to almost give away trips to Israel and, in return, require attendance in six adult study classes and a small gift to the annual fundraising campaign (there was no solicitation of funds in Israel). Most of the 40 or so couples who went were in their thirties and forties and were generally not involved in Jewish communal life.

During those trips and after, participants made many positive comments about how the trip had made them aware of their Jewish peoplehood. An example that typified many of the comments was from a person who tearfully expressed to the entire group that he had never been a religious or observant Jew and, as a result, always felt like an inferior Jew. But seeing the many kinds of Jews who live in Israel — especially the secular Jews who constitute the majority of Israeli Jewry — allowed him to say, "I now know I am a Jew and I am proud. This trip filled a void in me that I didn't even realize existed." I was deeply moved by his comment. I was also moved and saddened by a written evaluation that came from a Jew by choice (a person who had converted to Judaism). She wrote that as a result of the trip, she had gained a new and valued understanding of Jewish peoplehood. By seeing immigration to Israel from all over the world of Jews of every color and background, and also by meeting Israelis, she felt accepted as "one of the family" — a feeling she did not always receive from American Jews.

One need not go to Israel to feel Jewish peoplehood (though this is one of many reasons I always encourage people to go to Israel). I suspect many Jews feel this sense of peoplehood, even if they have never left their home city. I think this may be in part because, for countless generations, our non-Jewish neighbors did not give us the option to leave. They literally forced us into "peoplehood circles" — they were called ghettos. Today, as each of us defines ourselves, most of us are lucky enough to be able to choose not only where we live and travel, but also whether we want to include ourselves in the circle of Jewish peoplehood.

Even though we now have great freedoms of choice and ghettos are things of our past, for better and for worse, many of us continue to feel some of the sensations of physically living as one. By and large, I think it is for the better. As a kid I remember learning the concept of peoplehood in religious school in the saying, "All Jews are responsible one for the other." I had respect for the concept then, and I still do.

What about thinking about other people? That is also important to Judaism, as you will see in the next chapter.

Questions From This Chapter You May Wish to Ponder

- Rather than talking about "One People," how effective would the UJC's (the former UJA) fundraising be if they changed their slogan to "Hear O Israel, The Lord Our God, The Lord Is One"?

- What adjective(s) would you put in this blank: I feel _____ to be part of the Jewish people?

- What approach do you think is better for a healthy society: the Western emphasis on the individual or the Jewish emphasis on the community?

Chapter 6
"The Jewish Code of Behavior Is Out of Touch and Out of Date"

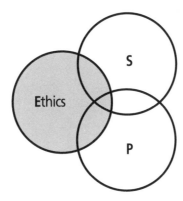

Jewish ritual and Jewish law are two of the last places most Jews today would look for guidance in conducting their day-to-day behavior: what to wear, what to eat, how to act at work, what to say to a friend, child, parent, and so on.

These are the kinds of decisions that consume most of our waking hours. Most people who spoke with me said that, for them, Judaism does not play much of a role in such matters. How could it? For the challenges and decisions that a modern person has to face, much of what Judaism has to say is out of touch and out of date for most of us, most of the time.

Or is it? How do you decide right from wrong? Does Judaism influence any of your decision making? This chapter explores how Jewish ethics and values influence the behavior of many Jews — even those whose formal Jewish education was terrible or nonexistent.

Also, in reviewing the relevance of Jewish thinking about how Jews should behave, this chapter looks at the rationale behind Jewish laws, ethics, and values. This rationale may both surprise and appeal to you.

Judy

Corporate law was her calling, and she has excelled in all aspects of her legal practice. At 46, Judy has become one of the most respected partners at her large firm. She graduated from Yale Law School and, upon graduation, steadily moved up the ranks of her profession. Currently, she is also an officer in her state's bar association. "I'm passionate about law — and that's not only because my husband is also a lawyer," she said with a laugh. "Seriously, I love the logic of law and the discipline it imposes, and at the same time, I love the challenge of working with the law to deal with situations that the law didn't exactly anticipate — which seems to be almost all situations." She thinks it is a shame that lawyers have been the subject of so many jokes and scorn "because almost every lawyer I've met has been a person of high integrity and honesty."

She is proud that Judaism has always placed a high value on its legal tradition but added, "in spite of that respect, for the most part, the Jewish code of law seems outdated and unnecessary to me. Modern democracies have systems of law that more or less seem to keep society civilized." Beyond that, she feels very comfortable with her Jewishness, though she does not practice a high level of observance. She did not have a bat mitzvah and said Judaism did not seem particularly important in her family, though they lived in a Jewish neighborhood. "In forming my Jewish identity, I would cite my years in my synagogue's youth group and a college summer program in Israel as pivotal and positive experiences for me."

She is a poised and secure person who speaks assertively. Listening to her, it is easy to imagine her speaking with authority to a judge or jury. Looking at her, you would never guess that she has been married almost 25 years and that she is the mother of three teenage children. They belong to a synagogue but only attend on the High Holidays or if they are invited to a bar mitzvah.

This, she explained, is because "in or out of the synagogue, I have to say that, except for the value of tradition, I find Jewish ritual life more or less meaningless for me."

Judy: I definitely consider myself to be Jewish, but I don't lead my life by Jewish law. I don't feel I have a need for Jewish law. I'll concede that I'm not very well versed in Jewish law. But I'm comfortable with that level of knowledge since my behavior is governed very well by a much more up-to-date system: American law.

Gil: *That may be the case, but I would suggest that your behavior is probably also a product of Jewish law.*

Judy: Well, I suppose you're right. There are Jewish things I do. My kids had bar mitzvahs, the boys were circumcised, we always go to Passover seders. That sort of thing.

Gil: *That's not what I meant. I am talking about day-to-day behavior that is distinctly Jewish.*

Judy: I hate to generalize, but I suppose there is some behavior that Jews seem to have in common with Jews.

Gil: *What are you referring to?*

Judy: Well, at the risk of sounding like an anti-Semite, I find Jews are critical and argumentative and controlling. But at the same time, on the plus side, I also think Jews are inquisitive, question the status quo, and are passionate. It's really two different ways of looking at the same behavior.

Gil: *I've heard that kind of sentiment before. Like I've heard people say that Jews are nagging and neurotic and phobic. A more generous description I've also heard is that Jews are caring, family-centered, and alert to danger — understandably.*

Judy: I guess beauty is in the eyes of the beholder. A person who loves Jews could cite the same behavior that an anti-Semite uses as ammunition. Though I can think of a pro and con that don't have flip sides. On the pro side, I'd put creativity and humor and a love of learning. On the negative side, I'd put materialism.

Gil: *Do you think that Jewish materialism is different from gentile materialism?*

Judy: Probably not. Now that we're talking about it, I must admit that many of the ardent "antimaterialists" of the counterculture seemed to have been Jews. See, that is why I did not want to generalize. Still, there does seem to be some "Jewish behavior."

Gil: *It does sometimes seem to me that Jews act this way or that. But I agree with your hesitation to generalize. It's not fair or right to think like that. After all, there are Jews I like and Jews I don't like — because of their individual behavior, not because they are Jewish. I would say the same of non-Jewish people.*

Judy: So wait a minute, if that is the case, how is any of this behavior a product of Jewish law?

Gil: *Well, the behavior of Jews varies a lot. Just look at the State of Israel or the Jews in your town. The degree to which people observe Jewish law also varies a lot. Still, I say that Jewish behavior is a product of Jewish law because Jewish law is a product of Jewish ethics and values. Those ethics and values have remained consistent and have been passed on for countless generations. After reflecting on the hundreds and hundreds of Jews I've met in my life, I've reached the conclusion that those values guide and influence a lot of Jewish behavior — even though I think many Jews today are probably unaware that Jewish ethics are behind a lot of their day-to-day behavior.*

Judy: I don't understand what you mean. There's almost something insulting about that statement.

Gil: *I meant no offense. Maybe I should have said that all people are influenced by their values — though on a regular basis, people seldom think about what values are behind their behavior. Our behavior is kind of "programmed" by the ethics and values we learn from our culture. I have a friend who calls this our "cultural DNA."*

Judy: Cultural DNA?

Gil: *It really just means that we get our ethics and values from the people around us — our families, our ethnic background, our country. They are passed down from generation to generation. It's not genetic, though, like the term DNA would imply. It's really learned behavior that gets taught from one generation to the next. Then those ethics and values become part of us.*

> ## "I think many Jews today are probably unaware that Jewish ethics are behind a lot of their day-to-day behavior."

Judy: That makes sense in theory, but in real life do you really think that happens?

Gil: *Yeah, I do. This is how it was explained to me: We learn the majority of our values as kids. Some are obvious, some are not. We pick them up when our parents and teachers tell us stories about our people or culture. Those stories teach and reinforce values and ethics that are usually quite old. Every culture has a master story made up of these unique stories.*

Judy: Master story? I don't understand.

Gil: *Every child in a culture usually knows the master story by the time they are 10 or so. In American culture, for example, all kids learn early on that our American master story includes chapters or unique stories about the Pilgrims and Thanksgiving, the Revolutionary War, the Wild West, the Civil War, being a "superpower," and so on. From these stories we get values and ethics that guide the way many Americans see themselves and the world.*

Judy: So are you saying that American cultural DNA would include values that are taught like independence, freedom, strength, and Yankee ingenuity? Do you mean to say that these values learned from the American master story then influence the way all Americans act?

Gil: *Not all Americans, but in general, yes, these are some of the values many Americans have learned to hold dear — even though, as I said, day to day we're not really conscious of these values. At the same time, we're also influenced by all the other cultures and subcultures and the individual families that we belong to. They all have their own unique stories too.*

Judy: But you just said that each of us is influenced by values from more than one culture. If that's so, don't you think it's difficult to generalize about how Jews behave?

Gil: *I think generalizing about how Jews behave is difficult and unfair. That's why I said it's more constructive to look at cultures and ethics that influence behavior. I do feel comfortable saying that Jewish people have some collective ethics. We have a rich culture of stories and an equally rich set of values and ethics that flow from those stories. They deeply influence us — some people more than others, of course.*

Judy: I'm Jewish and I don't even know what stories you're talking about. How could that deeply influence me?

"I've never thought about getting any Jewish values from the Passover story before. Frankly, to me the seder has always been mostly a bore."

Gil: *There are a number of Jewish stories I bet you do know. One story in particular that almost every Jew knows is the one we tell about ourselves every spring during the Passover seder.*

Judy: That we were once slaves in Egypt? How does that influence anything I do today?

Gil: *I'll give you an example. I have a Jewish friend who was telling me about a group he proudly supported. It's a social justice group that provides lawyers free of charge to poor people. While telling me this, he threw in, "Coincidentally, most of the lawyers there are Jewish." I said to him, "Do you really think that was a coincidence?"*

Judy: What does that have to do with the exodus from Egypt?

Gil: *A lot. There are a number of basic Jewish values that are deep within us from the Exodus story. First, we care about justice—about people treating other people unfairly. Second, we care about the poor and the downtrodden. I recently learned that the Bible mentions helping the stranger 26 different times, often reminding us of our experience in Egypt. I think one reason is to teach the value that Jews should be sensitive to the pain of any person who is disadvantaged. We also care about freedom. And a huge value Jews have picked up from the Exodus story is optimistic hope. In fact, the word "Hatikvah," which is the national anthem of Israel, means "the hope."*

Judy: I've never thought about getting any Jewish values from the Passover story before. Frankly, to me the seder has always been mostly a bore.

Gil: *That may be, but if you think about it for a second, our people have been telling the same Passover story for 30 centuries — sometimes that's how long my parents' seder seems to last. But the point of the seder is to tell the story. Why do you think that is? I think it's because, if a people tell the same story every year, over and over again for 3,000 years, the ethics in the story sink in — deeply, and that is the intention.*

Judy: That does make sense. I mean, Americans have been telling the story of Thanksgiving for just a few centuries, and every school kid knows the American value of religious freedom.

Gil: *When cultures tell and retell their stories starting with young children, the stories have great power. They are loaded with very influential ethics and vitamin C. Seriously, I realized how powerful the ritual of telling the Passover story is when I read in the 1990 National Jewish Population Survey that participating in a Passover seder is one of the most widely observed Jewish practices in America — even among Jews who are not strongly committed to Judaism.*

Judy: Really? Passover must be more compelling than I realized. But other than the Passover story, what Jewish stories are you talking about?

Gil: *You probably know most of the fundamental story. A lot of the Jewish story is in the Bible.*

Judy: The whole Bible? That's a lot to study.

Gil: *That's why Jews are supposed to study the Bible. But you can find many Jewish values just by looking at the most famous Bible stories. There are the early stories of Adam and Eve and Noah's ark. From them, among other things, Jews learn the value of all life and the importance of the environment.*

> **"I don't think a person needs to be Jewish, or any religion, for that matter, to lead an ethical life."**

From the story of the founding families — Abraham, Sarah, Isaac, Rebecca, and so on — we learn the high value we place on our children and families (and also how difficult families are to manage). Skipping way ahead, the prophets like Isaiah, Elijah, and many others taught all kinds of ethics — like looking out for the disadvantaged and speaking out against wrong and corruption, to name a few.

Judy: Time out. Are you saying we Jews get all of our ethics and values from a collection of Bible stories that are thousands of years old?

Gil: *No, that is just a part of our master story. Jumping ahead in the Jewish story, the Diaspora experience gave us a number of values that reinforced or altered values we picked up in the Bible. We also picked up new values, like a deep respect for learning. In this century, the Holocaust and the creation of the State of Israel have taught us many things, like the importance of being strong in order to take care of ourselves and the challenge of the moral use of power.*

Judy: I guess I do know these stories. I've never thought of them in terms of imparting values to me.

Gil: *Most Jews know the stories. But I don't think many Jews think very often of the "Jewish values" that they have picked up from these stories. For that matter, I never did either until I learned about master stories. But the more I've thought about it, the more I think that our Jewish cultural DNA is a good explanation of why there are so many Jews involved in organizations fighting for human rights, the environment, social services, social justice, universities, hospitals, children's medical centers. You could go on and on. As if this activity is not enough, the Jewish record of philanthropy has virtually no equal in the Western world.*

Judy: When I receive mail from these organizations, I do get a good feeling when I see Jewish names on the letterhead. There often seem to be a disproportionate number of Jewish names.

Gil: *Those names are just one example. I believe our Jewish master story touches us deeply by teaching us our sense of ethics.*

Judy: But there are non-Jews involved in these organizations also. I don't think a person needs to be Jewish, or any religion, for that matter, to lead an ethical life.

Gil: *Neither do I. I would never say that Judaism is the only source of ethics in the world. At the same time, I would say that a lot of what*

Western people call "ethical behavior" comes from the Jewish religion. Going a step beyond that, I don't think people realize how much their sense of right and wrong has been heavily influenced by thousands of years of Jewish ethics.

Judy: Don't you think that's a pretty bold thing to say?

Gil: *Not really. For example, take some basic Jewish ethics that I think most people would agree with. You shouldn't murder innocent people. You should give to charity. If you're married, you shouldn't sleep around. You shouldn't steal. You should treat animals with kindness. You should honestly pursue justice.*

Judy: What are you doing, just reading the Ten Commandments?

Gil: *Not exactly, but pretty much. Can you think of any ethics more Jewish than the Ten Commandments?*

Judy: But almost everybody believes them today.

Gil: *That's my point. In the West today, we have inherited a basic sense of right and wrong that was originally based on Jewish ethics.*

Judy: Well, if we have all inherited these ethics anyway, why do we need to attach "Jewish" to it anymore?

Gil: *Many people don't, but I think that's a shame because we should be proud of that huge contribution we have made to the world. I'd also say that there is a lot more to Jewish ethics than just the Ten Commandments. I believe the Jewish system of ethics offers the world a lot more than a basic sense of right and wrong.*

Judy: To that I have to say that being Jewish is no guarantee of ethical living. Nothing makes me angrier than watching Jewish people profess to pray and be righteous in the synagogue who then leave the doors and act unethically in their regular lives. Or they are prejudiced, using words like *shvartzes* and *goyim*. That's hypocrisy — it sure does not make the world a better place.

Gil: *According to what I've read, that's definitely not how Judaism says we should behave. It makes me angry too, not to mention embarrassed. I call it anti-Jewish. The rabbis called that kind of behavior desecrating God. I once read a story the rabbis tell of an observant jeweler who is engrossed in his daily prayer when a customer comes to his shop. The customer sees a gem and offers the jeweler 100 shekels for it. But the jeweler does not respond and continues to pray. The customer offers 200, then 300, and then in exasperation yells, "Four hundred shekels is my final offer!" The jeweler does not respond to any of the offers. Finally he finishes praying and tells the customer, "The gem is yours for 100 shekels." The customer is shocked. And the jeweler responds, "Before you came to my shop, I would have been pleased with a price of 100. If I were to take advantage of you because you became frustrated, my prayers are of no value." This behavior is admired by the rabbis.*

Judy: Legally speaking, from my point of view, the jeweler could charge the 400 shekels that the customer was prepared to pay and he would be acting within the law. The customer was not a victim of any legal fraud or misrepresentation.

Gil: *Under the American system of law.*

Judy: That is correct.

Gil: *So what do you think is the basis of the American system of law?*

Judy: In the final analysis, it is what we all learned in grade school, that all people are entitled to life, liberty, and the pursuit of happiness.

> **"Nothing makes me angrier than watching Jewish people profess to pray and be righteous in the synagogue who then leave the doors and act unethically in their regular lives."**

Gil: *That is certainly what I've learned. And as much as I embrace those values as an American and feel lucky to be an American, I also embrace the basis of Jewish ethics and laws, which I think is quite different.*

Judy: Then I'll ask you, what do you think is the basis of Jewish ethics and law?

Gil: *The pursuit of goodness.*

Judy: That's it?

Gil: *Simply put, that's it. Some people might prefer to say that the basis of Judaism is the pursuit of holiness. Either way you put it, the ultimate goal is the same: to make the world a better place. Judaism says the way to do that is to make people good.*

> **"The ultimate goal is… to make the world a better place. Judaism says the way to do that is to make people good."**

Judy: If that's true, then again I say, why do you need Judaism? There are a lot of gentiles and secular humanists who are good people.

Gil: *I wouldn't argue with that. But I like the Jewish system of ethics because I like what Judaism says about life. Plus, I think Judaism has a pragmatic and wise attitude about human nature.*

Judy: Okay. You have intrigued me. What does Judaism say about life?

Gil: *In most everything I've read and learned about Judaism, two main ideas about life keep coming up. One is an emphasis on life in this world — as opposed to the afterworld. The other is an emphasis on justice. They are closely related actually.*

Judy: I don't see the connection.

Gil: *I should say that Judaism does speak about an afterworld, but the thrust in Judaism is how we behave in this world. Which leads to the emphasis on justice. I think Judaism recognizes that life is not fair. Some people have good fortune, some do not. Some are sick, some are not. Every time I flick on CNN, I'm reminded that life is not fair. So Jews are told to work on making life more fair or more just — for everyone in the world.*

Judy: That "sounds" real nice — like the beauty contest winner who said her hobbies are world peace. Who could argue with any of that? But frankly, to me that just sounds like lovely rhetoric.

Gil: *That leads to the other aspect of Judaism I said I find attractive: Like you, Judaism has a realistic attitude about human nature.*

Judy: Thank you for the compliment. But I'm not sure why I received it.

Gil: *What I meant is that you and Judaism understand that talk is cheap. If you want results — and Judaism wants a more just world for results — you had better not count on rhetoric.*

Judy: If you're going to wait for faith to move people, you're also going to wait a long time.

Gil: *I completely agree — and so does Judaism. That's one of the reasons you can be a Jew and still have doubt about your faith in God. In the words of one rabbi, "Action is the touchstone of Judaism." Notice he did not say "faith." Judaism cares more about your behavior than your belief. Which again gets back to the Jewish attitude about human nature.*

> **"Behavior is more important in Judaism than belief. Judaism realizes that faith is difficult for many people."**

Judy: Well, you have certainly tantalized me. What is this "Jewish" attitude about human nature?

Gil: *It's pretty simple really — it's about human potential. Judaism says that we humans have the potential to be animal-like or divine.*

Judy: The animal part is clear, but divine?

Gil: *We can be "above" animals. We have a conscience. We can choose good over evil. We can create. I know this is going to sound high and mighty, but when we use our conscience and choose to do and create good, this is considered being "holy" in Jewish eyes.*

"To use the words of the song, "Where is the love?" Judaism is about obligation. Where is the compassion in Jewish law?"

Judy: So the Jewish idea is that we have the potential to be good?

Gil: *The answer is yes, but. This gets back to the Jewish attitude about human nature. Judaism says people have the potential to be good — but without laws, don't count on it happening.*

Judy: But what if a person does not believe in God or is not sure?

Gil: *That's why Judaism has laws. As I said a moment ago, behavior is more important in Judaism than belief. Judaism realizes that faith is difficult for many people. So Judaism says go ahead and search for faith. But while we're looking around, or even if we give up, Judaism says we're supposed to act like decent people... to obey Jewish laws of behavior — regardless of our faith. Another way to look at it is that Judaism tells us to act decently whether we "feel moved" to or not. I think the world would be a better place if everyone did that.*

Judy: You might be right, but I don't see how Jewish laws would make that happen. I mean, the laws of Judaism go on and on; they never seem to end. I think human potential and justice are great ideas, but Jewish laws seem so onerous, one obligation after another. You can't do this and you must do that. What about a little love and compassion? Christians seem to be so much more concerned with that than we are.

Gil: *I could see how you might say that, but as I've looked into Jewish laws, I've found over and over again that the Jewish pursuit of justice is very much driven by compassion.*

Judy: If that's so, it isn't obvious to me. Give me an example.

Gil: *An example that really blew me away has to do with the Jewish law about distributing* tzedakkah *to the poor. First, Judaism says there is no justice in having poor people and people with plenty. So to make the world more just, we should collect and distribute* tzedakkah.

Judy: That means charity, right?

Gil: *Yes and no.* Tzedakkah *is usually translated to mean "charity" — but actually the word comes from the Hebrew word for justice — tzedek. Giving* tzedakkah *in Judaism is an obligation by law. On the other hand, the word charity comes from the Latin word* caros, *which means love or endearment. Giving charity is voluntary, based on being moved by your heart to give.*

Judy: That's my point. To use the words of the song, "Where is the love?" Judaism is about obligation. Where is the compassion in Jewish law?

Gil: *Well, if you think in practical terms, you will have a lot more money to give to needy people if you obligate people by law to give* tzedakkah. *For the givers, that's not necessarily fun, but it's very loving of the needy.*

Judy: Hmmm, so you're saying to look at the motivation behind the laws —as we lawyers would say, the spirit of the law which in this case, you claim, is compassion.

Gil: *In many cases. The example that blew me away is even more striking — at least it is for me. Jewish law says that you should give more money to a rich man who has lost everything than to a poor person who never had anything.*

Judy: What? How is that compassionate? That seems almost cruel to the poor person.

Gil: *That was my reaction too — until I heard the explanation, or as you put it, the spirit behind the law. Based on American laws and values of equality, that does seem cruel. But the Jewish law in this case is based on who is in more pain, who is hurting more. And the rabbis felt that a rich person who had lost everything was suffering more than someone who never had anything. Like I said, that explanation just didn't jibe with my sense of values, but the more I thought about it, the more I realized that the rabbis may have thought differently about equality than I do, but they were motivated by compassion.*

> **"What about all the… laws of keeping kosher? …They're based on outdated health concerns. How does that make people achieve their potential for good?"**

Judy: It's interesting that the rabbis who wrote that law would try to put themselves in the shoes of the rich and the poor like that. Especially since I imagine most rabbis would not have known what having wealth would feel like.

Gil: *I suspect you're right. On top of that, they wouldn't know what a rich person who became poor feels like inside.*

Judy: Other than to know that it must feel terrible. That really is empathetic on their parts. Even though I'm not sure I would reach the same conclusion they did, I can see how their thinking is compassionate.

Gil: *Over and over, I've found that compassion and justice are intertwined in Jewish law. Judaism says that if we follow the law, we're elevating ourselves. If our actions are guided by these laws, we're on the road to achieving our potential for good—or as some would say, our potential to be holy.*

Judy: What about all the obligations and laws of keeping kosher? Those laws seem so foolish. They're based on outdated health concerns. How does that make people achieve their potential for good? And what does that have to do with compassion?

Gil: *I had also always thought that keeping kosher was based on health, trichinosis, indigestion, and who knows what else. When I did some checking, though, I found out that this is a widely held misconception. I even found a magazine describing this myth of keeping kosher in an article called "Soul Food Not Health Food."*

Judy: Health is the explanation that I've always heard. So what is keeping kosher about?

Gil: *The best explanation I've read is that the ideal behind keeping kosher is the same ideal behind most Jewish ethics and laws—to elevate us and maximize our potential to be good—with compassion behind it all.*

Judy: I still don't see what that has to do with what we can eat or not eat or how we should eat.

Gil: *The laws of keeping kosher are Judaism's way of elevating the act of eating. Have you ever watched a nature show where bigger, stronger animals rip apart a weaker animal and thought, "That poor animal— life is not fair."*

Judy: I have thought that. But that's life, I guess. Big fish eats little fish.

Gil: *In the animal kingdom that's life. But Jews are not supposed to be like animals. We're supposed to realize that killing an animal is not just. When we do kill, we're supposed to be compassionate and do it in a painless manner.*

Judy: I've heard that kosher slaughtering is cruel.

Gil: *There are people who think that. That's a controversy today in the Jewish world. But the whole reason there is a debate in the first place is because the Jewish goal is to avoid suffering and pain. This is not something animals think about when they are killing their prey. Plus, unlike the animal kingdom, we're not allowed to kill and eat any creature weaker than we are—which would include all animals.*

Judy: So why are some animals okay to eat and others not?

Gil: *No one knows for sure what the reason is. I've read a number of explanations. Most have to do with elevating us and making us more compassionate.*

Judy: For example?

Gil: *Well, one person I know who keeps kosher told me that when he keeps kosher, he has to think a lot about what he is eating. He likes that because it reminds him at every meal and snack of how lucky he is to have food and to be healthy enough to eat. Taken far beyond that is an interesting explanation I read, which said that the Jewish ideal is that we should be vegetarians.*

Judy: How does that explain that Jews can eat certain animals?

Gil: *The explanation says that Judaism believes killing animals isn't right. Even worse, to me, is the gruesome and cruel practice described in the Bible of ripping off and eating parts of a living animal. While seeing this as wrong, Judaism also realizes that asking everyone to be a vegetarian was not realistic. So the compromise is that we're restricted from eating some animals — and we can never eat a living animal.*

Judy: I can see the advance, but I still don't see how you get to vegetarianism.

Gil: *The Jewish thinking is that if we're conscious of everything we eat, as opposed to the way animals eat — they kill whatever they want and routinely eat living animals — eventually, we would conclude that eating and killing of any animal is wrong. Then, hopefully on our own, we would decide to become vegetarians.*

Judy: How wonderful that would be if everyone were a vegetarian. Too bad our desire for meat is so great. I do admire those who can go without, though personally I can't resist a good steak once in a while. Still, that's an interesting explanation. If you accept it, I can see how there is a connection between keeping kosher and ethics.

Gil: *This explanation is consistent with other things I've learned about keeping kosher. Like I learned that eating standing up is considered not kosher because we're acting like animals. Again, we're supposed to elevate ourselves.*

Judy: It's a good thing animals can't order from drive-throughs. I think I'm getting the idea.

Gil: *Even though we share much with animals, Judaism says we're different because we have a conscience. So here in the laws of keeping kosher we're reminded that we have the ability to choose good over evil — that we have the potential for good.*

> **"A group of rabbis ruled that the grapes picked by oppressed Chicano workers were not kosher. In effect, the rabbis were saying that eating those grapes was unethical."**

Judy: I don't think keeping kosher will guarantee that a person will be good.

Gil: *Me either, but this is another place where I think Judaism is pragmatic. Jews are supposed to always think about their potential for good. What better time to remember this than when we eat — something we all do, all the time? For example, I often eat standing up. Since learning what Judaism has to say about it, when I eat standing, I often find that I think about the Jewish teaching on the matter. It might only be for a fraction of a second, but I still think about it.*

Judy: Do you then sit down?

Gil: *All the diet books say I should too. Sometimes I do, but even when I don't, my consciousness has been raised — and I think that's the main point.*

Judy: I don't think I would think about it.

Gil: *That's what I thought, but I do find myself doing it anyway. I wouldn't be surprised if you find the same thing happening to you. I'll give you another example. Some years ago, a group of rabbis ruled that the grapes picked by oppressed Chicano workers were not kosher. In effect, the rabbis were saying that eating those grapes was unethical. That's because keeping kosher is ultimately about ethics. I still think about that story often when I eat grapes.*

Judy: I think I might now as well. I've never thought of the laws of keeping kosher in terms of making me a better person.

Gil: *One way I remember is that the word kosher has become part of American slang. If you look it up in* Webster's Dictionary, *it means proper or correct, as in "That deal was kosher."*

Judy: I never thought of kosher like that before. Now that you mention it, though, I've heard many people — Jews and non-Jews — use the word kosher to mean acting properly or ethically or "above board."

Gil: *That's at the core of all Jewish law. It's designed to make us better people. There are large bodies of law about how to behave ethically in business, how to treat the widow and the orphan, giving tzedakkah, caring for the ill, grieving families, and on and on. You name it, Judaism has a law about it.*

Judy: Some of that sounds great, but it seems that a lot of that law is out of touch and meaningless in today's world.

Gil: *Some of it is. For example, there are a number of laws about making sacrifices in the ancient temple. But most of the laws I've looked at have compelling rationales. Even for the laws that seem to be relics or irrelevant in the modern world, the spirit behind them has a lot of meaning. For example, I've heard good explanations of the spirit behind laws like keeping the Sabbath or eating matzah on Passover.*

Judy: So are you telling me that you observe all of those laws?

Gil: *No, not even close. But I think about the laws I do know, I often try them or parts of them, and I'm interested in learning more. Most of what I've learned has made me proud of our tradition—even though I recognize I'm not observing a lot of Jewish laws.*

Judy: Don't you feel like a hypocrite?

Gil: *No, I feel like a serious Jew. I actively struggle with what I think is the right thing to do, the wrong thing, and in between. I like the idea of trying to become a better person. I really like the Jewish idea that we humans have tremendous potential for good.*

Judy: But still, to achieve your potential seems almost impossible. It seems Judaism gives you a choice of becoming a perfectionist or a hypocrite.

> **"To achieve your potential seems almost impossible. It seems Judaism gives you a choice of becoming a perfectionist or a hypocrite."**

Gil: *Judaism recognizes that we humans are not perfect — and never will be. At the same time, we're told we have the potential to be better — so we should try to elevate ourselves.*

Judy: It still seems to me that if, for example, you're obeying some rules of keeping kosher and not others, that's hypocrisy.

Gil: *I had a teacher once who said obeying Jewish law is like obeying traffic laws. He said you should always strive to uphold traffic laws — even if sometimes you might speed. Plus, he pointed out, there is a difference between speeding at 95 mph and 70 mph. If you truly strive to uphold the law but sometimes break some laws to some degree, don't think of yourself as a hypocrite... think of yourself as being human. At the same time, of course, keep trying to do better.*

Judy: I suppose there is something to be said for that. So often it seems like the choice is to observe or violate the law.

Gil: *But most of the time life is not so black or white. I do my best to use Jewish values, ethics, and laws as navigational tools on the road to being a good person — even if I may break some traffic laws.*

Judy: I guess your attitude is realistic. I will admit I do break some laws to some degree, but in general I still consider myself to be a law-abiding citizen.

Gil: *Even though I know I fall far short and violate many laws, I strive to be a law-abiding Jew for the same reason I strive to be a law-abiding citizen — all in all, I believe in the system. I really like the core values and ethics that are the foundation of the Jewish system.*

> **"I do my best to use Jewish values, ethics, and laws as navigational tools on the road to being a good person — even if I may break some traffic laws."**

Judy: I think I probably do too—though I'm not sure I knew that before. I never realized how ingrained these values and ethics are in me. I think you may be right that my being Jewish or my Jewish master story has affected a lot of what I think is right or wrong and what I think is important—not to mention what I think tastes good—I must say the idea of a hamburger and a glass of milk grosses me out. I also like what you have told me about the Jewish attitude about our potential for good.

Gil: *After all is said and done, striving to realize our potential for good is ultimately what I think being Jewish is all about. I like that. If everyone did that, what a world we would live in. When I combine this goal with a system of ethics and laws that is based on compassion and justice, I'm proud to be Jewish.*

Judy: Maybe the Jewish philosophy and system of striving to be better people is why I've wanted to pass Judaism on to my kids. I don't think I was consciously aware of that before. From what I know, I still prefer the American system of values and laws. But there appears to be much more to the Jewish system of laws and ethics than I discerned before. I could see merit in learning more about them.

Key Points to Hold Onto

Chapter 6: "The Jewish Code of Behavior Is Out of Touch and Out of Date"

- Jewish behavior varies a lot. What remains the same are the Jewish values and ethics that influence that behavior.

- All groups, including Jews, have a master story that imparts values and ethics to their members. These values are taught through the generations and influence behavior.

Key Points to Hold Onto (continued)

Chapter 6: "The Jewish Code of Behavior
Is Out of Touch and Out of Date"

- The Jewish master story has imparted many values to many Jews. Some of those values are an emphasis on: justice, families and children, care for the disadvantaged, freedom, hope and optimism, speaking out against wrong, reverence for learning, and the importance of being strong.

- The Western world has inherited a basic sense of right and wrong that is largely based on Jewish ethics.

- Judaism says people have the potential to behave like animals or like the divine.

- The basis of Jewish ethics and law is the pursuit of goodness. To realize our potential for good, Judaism relies on laws.

- Judaism cares more about behavior than belief — so Jews are expected to behave with decency and obey laws regardless of their level of belief or nonbelief in God.

- Judaism recognizes that life is not fair and consequently emphasizes justice.

- The Jewish pursuit of justice is based on the values of love and compassion — though that spirit of the law may not be obvious by looking literally at Jewish law. The laws of giving *tzedakkah* and keeping kosher are examples.

- If you break laws while striving to uphold them, think of yourself, not as a hypocrite, but as a serious Jew who is not perfect or divine — you are human with much potential for good.

Afterthoughts

There is one very important misconception about Jewish behavior that I think is worth mentioning again here. It is the misconception that somehow Jewish behavior is not authentic if faith in God is weak or absent. Stated as a question: Can a person really behave Jewishly if they don't believe in God? Our rabbinic scholars had this to say on the subject in the Talmud, their revered collection of Jewish law: God is quoted as saying, "If only my children would forget about me and keep my laws." To me, the reading of this passage is clear: Judaism places proper behavior before belief. Whether you believe in God or not, Judaism expects you to act like a *mensch* — with decency.

Of course, you could then ask, What is decency? Judaism has much to say about this subject, and this chapter purposefully did not get into a lot of specifics. There are literally so many volumes of Jewish thought about decent behavior that you could spend the rest of your life studying and never finish.

For example, a short (500-plus-page) collection of Jewish ethics and ideals for everyday living called *Voices of Wisdom* (edited by Francine Klagsbrun) offers hundreds of passages. Just to give you a little sampler, here are some of the entries: Controlling your Temper, Striking a Balance Between Humility and Arrogance, The Value of Friendship, Returning Lost Property, Forgiving Your Enemies, Getting Along With In-laws, Stern vs. Permissive Discipline, Physicians' Responsibilities, Student-Teacher Relationships, Responsibilities of Employers, The Ethics of the Marketplace, Attitudes Toward War, Showing Kindness to Animals, Placing Life Above Laws, and Rights of the Accused.

You get the idea. They almost sound like the names of articles you would see on the covers of popular magazines at the grocery store. Some of the media now seem to be into ethical behavior; in fact, they have coined the phrase "a random act of kindness" to highlight rare examples of kind and decent behavior. I've been struck by this phrase, as I imagine our rabbis over the ages would be, because Judaism says kindness and decency should be routine, not random. Judaism is about making our lives civilized through "regular acts of kindness."

As I read examples in Ms. Klagsbrun's book of behavior that our rabbis and other Jewish thinkers thought should be decent, civilized, "regular acts of kindness" — I was not startled by their thinking (though I can't say I agreed with all of it). Most of their suggestions I more or less expected to find. This is because these thinkers were guided by the same Jewish ethics and values that I have gleaned and embraced as I have grown up. I believe most Jews have picked up and adopted many of them as well.

Speaking for myself, I find the ethics and values of Judaism inspiring and pragmatic. In particular, I am referring to the values of: striving to make the world a better place, pursuing goodness, pursuing justice, and treating all living creatures with compassion. Not only am I attracted to these values, but also — as I daily watch human cruelty and savagery on the news or read of yet another immoral dealing in politics or business — I find these ethics as badly needed and relevant in our day as ever.

Questions From This Chapter You May Wish to Ponder

- As you reflect on your own upbringing and your personal master story, what people and stories influenced your attitude and values about:
  - getting an education,
  - treating your parents,
  - helping those less fortunate than you are,
  - working ethically?

- Was there anything in what you learned that you can attribute to being Jewish?

Chapter 7
"Hebrew School Was Worthless and Boring"

Raise your hand if your Jewish education was lousy. If this includes you, then you are joining the majority of people who spoke with me.

I heard from most people that their formal Jewish education consisted of bar/bat mitzvah or confirmation preparation. This meant mostly trying to learn to read Hebrew and chant some prayers — skills that were often not learned at all or poorly learned and quickly forgotten.

The contents of the previous chapters of this book — namely, defining Judaism and looking into Jewish ethics, spirituality, and peoplehood — are the subjects people told me they wished they had learned when they were in religious school.

Though millions and millions of dollars have been spent to educate Jews, and the intentions of most Jewish educators have been wonderful, it seems that most Jewish schools are at best an expensive social program for Jewish youth and at worst little more than inefficient bar/bat mitzvah factories. This chapter examines the issue of the failings and potential of Jewish education.

Dan

Dan says he has lived two different lives. He is a big, imposing, but very gentle figure. Meeting him today in his loose-fitting cotton pants and short-sleeved shirt, it is hard to imagine him wearing a white shirt and tie, leading a completely different lifestyle. He describes that lifestyle as his relatively conventional first life. Immediately after college he got a well-paying job as an electrical engineer. He married a woman who, like him, "was born Jewish but that's about it." They met in college, married at the age of 22, and bought a small home in the suburbs. Five years later they were divorced. They had no children and the marriage ended civilly. Dan and his ex are still friendly with each other.

Dan says his second life probably began shortly after he graduated from college. He discovered that he did not enjoy engineering in the corporate world and began to reevaluate many parts of his life. In the process, he and his wife began drifting apart. "We seemed to have very different values. She knew more or less what direction she wanted her life to take. I thought I did too when we met and while I was in school. But I found I was doing a lot of searching and that I was unsure. At first, my wife was supportive, but eventually it became clear that we wanted different things for our lives."

His searching led him on a journey that included exploring Eastern religions, backpacking through Asia, an unplanned nine-month stay as a volunteer on a kibbutz in Israel (which he loved), and going back to school, where he got a degree in elementary education.

Today, at 35, Dan has found contentment as a sixth-grade teacher. He does not have a significant other, though he dates a lot—Jews and non-Jews. He would like to remarry and have children when the right person comes along. He thinks the right person will probably "but not for sure" be Jewish, because in all of his searching he has found Judaism to be the "system I'm most attracted to, and I would like my children to know Judaism."

He would not have felt that way based on what he learned about Judaism growing up, however. "I don't want my kids to learn about Judaism the way I was taught." He considers his attraction to Judaism a part of his new second life. Based on his experiences, he feels Jewish education needs a lot of help, "probably a complete overhaul!"

Dan: Hebrew school was the biggest bore. I didn't learn anything. To me, that's sad; it shouldn't have been like that. I mean, the things I've learned about Judaism as an adult have been fascinating and valuable to me. Why didn't anyone ever teach me any of that when I was in religious school?

Gil: *Well, I know one reason why I didn't learn much. My friends and I thought of Hebrew school as social time. On top of that, we were complete devils... once during class I remember we threw furniture out of a second-story window. What a riot. It was like a riot. And for the most part, we knew that many of our parents really didn't care that much — mine did, of course.*

Dan: We were not quite that awful, but to say the least, my friends and I were not model students either. Of course, we were forced to go to religious school, so you can imagine what kind of motivated students we were. Still, I think we would have behaved a lot better if the material had been more interesting and the teachers weren't so terrible.

Gil: *In retrospect, some of my teachers were okay. I think a big problem was the curriculum. Like the emphasis on Hebrew. Trying to teach Hebrew in just a few hours a week was hopeless. I'm not sure why they even tried.*

> **"I wish I had been taught why I was having a bar mitzvah, not just how to have one."**

Dan: I believe trying to teach a few words of conversation and how to read a foreign alphabet is of marginal value. To me, that is not a method of teaching that will produce retainable and valuable knowledge.

Gil: *It's especially futile when the kids know that they are stuck in Hebrew school while all of their friends are home playing or in Little League.*

Dan: That competition for time is always going to exist. So, given the precious few hours we have to teach most kids, if it were up to me, I'd be teaching more about the values and spirit behind the law versus the letter of the law. Like for my bar mitzvah, I learned how to perform and chant — sort of, that is — but I didn't understand why I was even having a bar mitzvah. I wish I had been taught why I was having a bar mitzvah, not just how to have one.

Gil: *I agree with you. In my opinion, far too much time is spent teaching how Jews do things as opposed to why we do things. Skills training versus values training. I think that too often the values training is missing completely. Now if you combine the two, you have a memorable and powerful learning experience.*

Dan: That is the way I like to teach. Unfortunately, when I was in religious school that is not how I was taught. I learned a lot of "hows" that to a kid seemed dumb or outdated — frankly, even as an adult, some of the "hows" seem that way to me. But also as an adult, I've learned many wonderful "whys" of Judaism are behind most of the "hows."

Gil: *For example?*

Dan: Well, one example would be the Sabbath — not that I observe the Sabbath. Still, as a kid I learned that there seem to be a zillion laws and prohibitions about the Sabbath — you know: don't ride, don't work, don't write, don't touch money. When I was younger, no one ever told me that protecting the environment is one of the reasons behind these laws.

> **"If kids are going to really learn and accept their Judaism... they need credible explanations. ...they [also] need to be taught some realistic ideas about God and spirituality."**

Gil: *I didn't learn that until I was an adult either. For that matter, as an adult, I've learned that Judaism is very concerned with the environment. In fact, I recently found that there is a national organization that publishes all kinds of great material about Judaism and the environment.*

Dan: I spend a lot of time in my public school classes teaching my kids about the environment—they eat it up. Jewish kids would probably think it's cool that Judaism cares about it, too. But more than being "cool," it would be important for them to know that about Judaism.

Gil: *I think so. I think that not only would they find it interesting, they would find it appealing and relevant and a reason to be proud to be Jewish. As opposed to what you and I were taught: the prohibitions of the Sabbath. I think most kids—and adults—dismiss that as old-fashioned craziness.*

Dan: We don't give kids enough credit—they're pretty smart. I believe kids can not only handle explanations, they need explanations—the "whys"—they seem to crave that. If the explanation makes sense, they'll buy it. If my explanation is weak, or worse, if they are just told with no explanation that "that's just the way things are done," they just reject my idea. They may not say so, but I can tell they are thinking, as you put it, that what I'm telling them is "craziness, but we gotta do it, 'cause the teacher says so."

Gil: *I agree, kids are smart little critters. I watch in amazement how they manipulate adults, especially their parents.*

Dan: They can be very critical thinkers as well. From an educational point of view, if kids are going to really learn and accept their Judaism, I'm with you, they need credible explanations. I also think they need to be taught some realistic ideas about God and spirituality.

Gil: *Maybe a kid in nursery school can only handle an image of an old man with a gray beard as God. But I think older kids—and probably the younger ones as well—deserve and can handle much more than that. I've seen books that do a wonderful job of talking to kids about spirituality and God.*

Dan: I've also seen some great kids' books that were simple, yet even I found them stimulating. This is also what Jewish education should be emphasizing. But I've got to tell you, as a teacher, it's not realistic to expect a school to accomplish a lot unless the parents are on board.

Gil: *I don't think that will happen with Jewish education unless Jewish parents are more excited about wanting Judaism for their kids and reinforcing that in their homes and lives. I believe that children need memories of good Jewish experiences for Judaism to stick. Much of that has to come from their parents.*

Dan: How do you do that? It seems most Jewish parents had fairly lean Jewish upbringings and crummy Jewish educations themselves. How do you get them excited and motivated to create good Jewish memories for their kids after that?

Gil: *It's not easy. It may not be possible for everyone. Still, I think it is possible. If people are willing and open, they can find much in Judaism to get excited about. From what people have told me, major life events are when they seem most open and willing to examine or reexamine their Judaism — like the birth or bar or bat mitzvah of a child, the death or illness of a parent, or a trip to Israel as an adult.*

Dan: In my case, it was a career change and a divorce. It took a lot of searching — and Judaism was not one of the places I originally searched. But eventually I did conclude that Judaism had much to offer me and is worth perpetuating. That's why I say, when I have my own kids some day, I want them to know Judaism.

Gil: *I reached a similar conclusion, not just because I think Judaism had something for me, but also because I think Jews and Judaism have given the world so much. I think we have made the world a more civilized place.*

Dan: Don't you think that's a little overstated?

Gil: *I admit that it sounds grandiose. But here is how I came to that conclusion: Most of Jewish history is filled with stories of our neighbors hating and hurting us in terrible ways. Combine that with the fact that we're a tiny sliver of the humanity that has inhabited earth. In spite of those two facts, we have given the world incredible achievements in almost all walks of life.*

Dan: How about sports?

Gil: *I did say "almost." Actually there are good examples in sports, but if you want, skip that one, look at music, literature, law, journalism, the physical and social sciences, medicine, psychology, technology. I could go on and on. Even Mark Twain noted our contributions.*

> **"Judaism is like a diamond. Every time you shine a light on it, different facets will reflect back at you."**

Dan: The Mark Twain as in *Huckleberry Finn*?

Gil: *The same one. I read an essay of his written in the late 1800s where he said that our numbers are so tiny that we're like stardust in the Milky Way. In spite of our tiny numbers, he marveled that Jews have made huge, disproportionate contributions to the world in every realm — and as he put it, we did all this with our hands tied behind our backs. I read recently that Jews are about ⅓ of 1 percent of the world's population, but we're the holders of 18 percent of all Nobel prizes ever awarded. I find that mind-boggling.*

Dan: That is mind-boggling, especially if I step away and try to objectively observe what has happened to Jews over the centuries. Logically I would predict that at worst we would be gone by now, at best we would be a bitter, downtrodden people. Really, it is amazing that we have become the opposite — an optimistic people that has contributed and achieved so much. If more Jews thought about that, that alone could be a reason to become more excited about Judaism.

Gil: *I'd say it's a reason to be proud. But there is so much more to Judaism. I heard once that Judaism is like a diamond. Every time you shine a light on it, different facets will reflect back at you.*

Dan: That's good. But still, I get back to the question: How do you get Jews interested in shining a light on the diamond in the first place?

Gil: *I think they would be interested if more time was spent giving Jews answers to the question: Why should I be Jewish? And those answers should use terms and concepts that people today can relate to.*

Dan: Like what?

Gil: *Like talking about Judaism as a rich way of life that you can enter through what I call Jewish E.S.P.: Jewish ethics, Jewish spirituality, and Jewish peoplehood.*

Dan: I've never heard Judaism described or defined in those terms before.

Gil: *They may be new terms, but the ideas are quite old.*

Dan: What do you mean?

Gil: *Traditionally, the three components of Judaism —*
ethics, spirituality, and peoplehood *— have always been emphasized as sacred. But for generations our rabbis and texts have used three different words: Torah, God, and Israel.*

> **"Traditionally, the three components of Judaism — ethics, spirituality, and peoplehood — have been emphasized as sacred. But for generations our rabbis and texts have used three different words: Torah, God, and Israel."**

Dan: I can relate better to your words.

Gil: *Me, too, that's why I use them — but they are really the same thing. Part of teaching Jews today should be using the words of today.*

Dan: In education, that's fairly obvious — at least it is in secular education. After all, we no longer teach English using the language of Shakespeare or Chaucer. Yet we do still teach about the work of these authors.

Gil: *If we use language that people will understand, we can still teach about great works. But if people can't relate to the language, the great work doesn't seem so great.*

Dan: All children's books and teaching are examples of that. For that matter, all effective education is. You take challenging material and make it understandable, relevant, and personal. It seems like common sense, but it also just seems to be missing in Jewish education.

> **"Effective education is [taking] challenging material and [making] it understandable, relevant, and personal. It seems like common sense, but it also seems to be missing in Jewish education."**

Gil: *It shouldn't be, though. To use your words, I've found very understandable, relevant, and personal answers to the question: Why be Jewish?*

Dan: How do you answer?

Gil: *I've come up with different answers. In philosophical terms, I like Judaism's belief in the great potential of people to do and be good. More personally, I tell myself and my kids that Judaism makes me proud, it makes me think, it makes me feel connected, it gives me guidance to be a better person, and when I'm lost or lonely, it gives me roots and comfort. And it always gives me family and extended family. All in all, it helps give my life meaning. As my kids have gotten older, I've also told them that I don't know if it's the best system in the world, but I think it's an incredibly good and intelligent system, and I feel lucky to call it mine. I want it to belong to my kids too.*

Dan: I don't feel I've studied Judaism enough to be able to say all that. But I will say, whenever I've looked into something Jewish, I've found a tremendous amount of careful thought and wisdom.

Gil: *That is what I've concluded, and I say that based on asking one heck of a lot of questions about Judaism in recent years: hard ones, simple ones, angry ones, dumb ones, rebellious ones. In the process, I've also learned that asking questions is very Jewish.*

Dan: That's another thing I've found that, as a teacher, I especially like —Judaism has great respect for questions and critical thinking.

Gil: *That's true. I've always admired that traditional Jewish study is with a partner, to encourage questions and critique. Personally, I love to ask questions and I ask anyone. I asked you questions. I've asked relatives, friends, teachers, authors, rabbis. I've been amazed — most people are more than willing to answer and share their opinions. I think offering opinions must be Jewish too. Anyway, I've also found a lot of answers and even more questions in books.*

Dan: I don't mind asking questions, but when it comes to reading, I'm buried. I always have a pile of things waiting for me that I'm behind on. I barely seem to get through the daily newspaper.

Gil: *I could probably save you a lot of time and work by sending you the names of a few of the places where I've found some of the best answers — written concisely in plain English. If you're interested, you can take a look at whatever you have time for.*

Dan: I'd appreciate that.

Key Points to Hold Onto

Chapter 7: "Hebrew School Was Worthless and Boring"

- Trying to teach the Hebrew language in a few hours a week is not likely to succeed.

- We should spend a lot more time teaching "Why be Jewish" versus "How to be Jewish." For example, children should learn "why" they are having a bar/bat mitzvah, not just "how" to chant or perform for their bar/bat mitzvah.

- Children should be shown that Judaism is relevant and valuable — for example, the wonderful Jewish values about the environment.

- Children should be taught about Jewish spirituality in meaningful ways.

- For Jewish education to work, parents must be supportive and reinforce Judaism at home and in life.

- Adults and children should be shown that Judaism is multifaceted, rich, and has made huge contributions to the world.

- This richness has three places you can enter: Ethics, Spirituality, and Peoplehood. These are modern words that Jews today may have an easier time relating to than the traditional words: Torah, God, and Israel.

- Questioning is a key to learning more about Judaism. To question is very Jewish.

Afterthoughts

Many people told me that they could relate to the topics discussed in this chapter. (Not only that, on two separate occasions, single women asked me if Dan was "available" — no joke!) The need for quality Jewish education (and men) is obvious.

As the chapter mentioned, Jewish education has problems with curriculum, some teachers, and too much emphasis on teaching how to be Jewish versus why be Jewish. Those problems are hard for most of us to impact immediately and change — though we should try. We need to be talking to principals, teachers, and boards and demanding quality.

There is a problem that we can have an impact on immediately: us. I believe that one of the serious problems facing Jewish education is parental support or lack thereof. Far too many parents do not push their kids to acquire Jewish knowledge. After all, we never saw any value in it, and in the final analysis, to get into a good college, your grades from Hebrew school are of no consequence. When I was in Hebrew school — and I have heard this remains the case today — parents allowed their kids to behave in ways that they would never tolerate in secular school. Plus, many parents feel that going to a second school after school robs their children of valuable extracurricular opportunities.

One parent told me a story of his kid telling him he hated "Talmud Torture" (as opposed to the correct name for the school: Talmud Torah) and wanted to quit. His response was, "I hated Talmud Torture, too, and when I told my father, he said he hated it, too, but he had to go. I had to go, and so do you." Even without being this explicit, kids can tell how their parents feel, and consequently, the chances of acquiring much in religious school are low.

This scenario reminds me of a lesson about how parents should transmit Judaism to their children that I heard from Dr. Ron Wolfson from the University of Judaism. He said he was on an airplane and gave some thought to the instructions routinely given by the flight attendant that "in the event of sudden cabin decompression, an oxygen mask will fall out of the panel in front of you… blah, blah, blah." The part that got his attention was: "If you are traveling with young children, place your mask on first before attending to your child."

At first blush, this instruction is counterintuitive. We always tend to our children first — especially in cases of emergency. Of course we all understand why in this case we must put our mask on first. If we were to pass out, there would be no hope for either ourselves or our children. Plus, we must model for our children that placing a mask on your face is not scary — in fact, it's a must.

The same is true for showing our children that we see value in Judaism. If we don't breathe Judaism, then neither will our kids. What we model at home and in our conversations in front of our kids is critical. When people told me of their fond memories of learning about Judaism, most revolved around family traditions, routines, and customs that they cherished. I should add that several people also appreciated that their parents had sent them to Jewish summer camps, where they had positive Jewish educational experiences.

If we want our children to perpetuate Judaism — and many people told me that they did want that — then we must personally take the steps necessary to show our kids how. It might mean learning with our kids. (By the by, for several years I took piano lessons together with my son. It was fun and most rewarding to study together. To prepare for his bar mitzvah, I hired a teacher and we spent several months studying his bar mitzvah Torah portion together in English. That was even more rewarding!) We need to say and do things that show our kids that we value Judaism as much as we value math, literature, science — piano — and the other sources of knowledge we feel our children should have to lead good and productive lives.

Again, I want to say that the steps, if any, that you care to take are a personal decision. If you are interested, some suggestions are listed on the next couple of pages.

Questions From This Chapter You May Wish to Ponder

- How would you like your children's or grandchildren's Jewish education to be different from yours?

- What would you need to do to make sure it was different?

- What knowledge do you believe is most important for children to learn for them to lead a life that is both good and productive?

Gil Mann
c/o Leo & Sons Publishing
175 Oregon Avenue South
Minneapolis, MN 55426

Fax: 763-542-0171
E-Mail: MannGil@aol.com
Website: www.BeingJewish.org

Dear Dan:

Thanks for speaking with me the other day. I appreciated hearing your point of view. As I promised you, I went to my computer, files, and bookshelves to find some things for you to look at that I thought you would like.

I found so many quality options that I had a hard time deciding what to choose. There's lots more where this came from, but here are a few highlights that I found inviting.

Again, this is by no means a complete list; still, this is a pretty good start. You can also find this material and much more on my website, **www.BeingJewish.org** (click on links). I have found these materials and organizations to be engaging, inspiring, and thought-provoking. I hope you do too.

Talk to you soon,

Gil

P.S. FYI, I included 2 good quotes (one written by a non-Jew, by the way) that I thought added some insight to our "Why be Jewish?" discussion. They're a little on the lofty side, still, I liked them — see what you think.

Super Short Bibliography of Good Jewish Places to Explore

Books

To Life, by Harold Kushner, published by Little and Brown

> A very readable, sensible, and enjoyable explanation of Judaism, by the author of *When Bad Things Happen to Good People*. This book is especially good for anyone who had a bad Hebrew school experience.

The Nine Questions People Ask About Judaism, by Dennis Prager and Joseph Telushkin, published by Touchstone, Simon & Schuster

> A skeptic's guide to Judaism that answers questions such as: Why do we need organized religion? How does Judaism differ from Christianity, Marxism, Communism, and Humanism? and seven more tough questions.

Celebrate! The Complete Jewish Holidays Handbook, by Lesli Koppelman Ross, published by Jason Aronson

> A nondenominational reference guide that has enough information in it to keep you going forever. This book explains many of the "hows" as well as the "whys" behind Jewish celebrations and traditions. Great for families — offers further reading options for kids and adults.

Jewish Literacy, by Joseph Telushkin, published by Morrow

> 346 brief entries on the essentials of Judaism, organized by subject. This plain English and entertaining book is a tremendous source of knowledge. Looking up one entry, it's easy to get caught up reading entry after entry — it's like eating Frito Lay potato chips — bet you can't read just one!

It's a Mitzvah! Step by Step to Jewish Living, by Bradley Artson, published by Behrman House

> If you think the Jewish code of behavior is outdated, this book will change your mind. It offers hundreds of modern, meaningful, and practical ways to practice Judaism — from protecting the environment to helping the homeless. It covers traditional ritual practices as well. As a bonus, it is filled with wonderful photos.

For a helpful catalog of Jewish books, send $5.00 and request *How to Build Your Home Jewish Library* from:

> Jewish Book Council
> 15 East 26th St.
> New York, NY 10010
> Web: http//www.jewishbookscouncil.org

Internet

There are thousands of Jewish "places to visit" on the internet. One way to start is to go to the Jewish search engine: www.maven.co.il

The first place I invite you to explore is the website based on this book:

www.BeingJewish.org

As a result of my work on this book and the thousands of emails I have received since it was first published, I know that many people are searching for ways to find more meaning and relevance in Judaism. Through my website, I hope to help, by providing friendly and inviting articles, ideas and resources. Also posted here is a column I write called Jewish Email of the Week, that is a public response to an anonymous email sent to me. Everything on my site is designed to allow you to easily access the three components of the Jewish Way of Life covered in this book: Ethics, Spirituality, and Peoplehood. Please come visit!

While you can discover countless Jewish websites on your own, I will recommend six of them:

www.ujc.org/ir_home.html

If you are looking for Jewish community and Jewish organizations, this site has a huge number of resources. You can search geographically or by interest. Contacts can be found here for everything from circumcisions to Jewish Federations to youth groups and many things in between. This site is a wonderful place to help you connect.

www.myjewishlearning.com

Want to learn more about Judaism or find some "how to" information? You're in luck! A lot of resources have gone into this site to provide you with information (and even courses) on a myriad of Jewish topics. Major categories include holidays, lifecycle, text, ideas and belief, culture, daily life, practice, and history. This site offers something for everyone whether, you're insecure about your level of Jewish knowledge or want to add to your knowledge base — and you can do your learning from the comfort of home!

www.jewishfamily.com

This is a great Jewish online magazine you may want to check out called Jewish Family Life. It has articles about parenting, answers to children's questions about Judaism (like "Can I visit Santa at the Mall?") interviews with famous Jews, areas about food, travel, etc. You can also interact with the magazine and other readers through your computer.

www.convert.org

> If you know somebody who is interested in converting to Judaism — or you simply want to learn more about Judaism — this welcoming site is a great place to start. Here you will find information about the differences between Judaism and Christianity, dealing with sensitive relationship issues, the names of over 70 rabbis of all denominations who perform conversions, and much more.

www.interfaithfamily.com

> Well known today is the phenomenon of Jews marrying non-Jews. This website candidly addresses the challenges faced by intermarried families and their extended families (like in-laws and grandparents). The site offers a Jewish perspective while respecting the faith of others. Look here for resources and links covering many topics like religious holidays, lifecycle events, outreach programming, and more.

www.Jewish.com

> This general Jewish site has a wide range of Jewish information covering many aspects of Judaism. Some of the topics you can pursue here are holiday information, ask a rabbi, recipes, book reviews, Jewish news, and more. They post many columns I have written in response to questions readers have emailed to me. To find these columns, enter "Gil Mann" in their search feature. They also have a Jewish store as a part of their site so you can find a Jewish gift for yourself or others.

Magazines

The Jerusalem Report

> Every 2 weeks this wonderful magazine comes out, and I can't wait to read it. Offering a clear and inviting format similar to *Time* or *Newsweek*, they cover the Jewish world like no one else—especially when it comes to news about Israel. You can count on their news, photographs, reviews, and columnists to provide valuable and thought-provoking insights into the Jewish world. To subscribe, contact:

> The Jerusalem Report
> P.O. Box 420235
> Palm Coast, FL 32142-0235
> 1-800-827-1119
> Web: www.jrep.com

Moment

If you want to delve deeper into modern Jewish subjects, this high-quality magazine is for you. In a serious but easy to read format, they examine such issues as "Is Hollywood Too Jewish?" "Right and Left Positions on The Middle East Peace Process," "Bridging the Gap Between American and Israeli Jews," and many others. They also have regular features like reviews, columns, and articles about Jewish Holidays. To subscribe contact:

Moment
4710 41st Street N.W.
Washington, D.C. 20016
1-800-777-1005
Web: http//www.momentmag.com

Video and Multimedia

The Jewish Video Catalog from Ergo Media, Inc.

Ergo has come up with an impressive assortment of Jewish videos. They also offer Judaica on CD-ROM for your computer. The variety of topics covers the gamut from history to cooking to drama. Many of their offerings are award winners. Regardless of your interests, you are bound to find something in their catalog that catches your attention. For a free catalog, contact them at:

Ergo Media, Inc.
668 American Legion Drive
P.O. Box 2037
Teaneck, NJ 07666-1437
1-800-695-3746
Fax: 201-692-0663
Web: http//www.jewishvideo.com

Kids' Stuff

Kids' Videos

Get the Israel Sesame Street videos (English) for your kids and yourself. As Tony the Tiger would say, "they're great!"

> Sisu Entertainment
> 18 West 27th St., 10th Floor
> New York, NY 10001
> Contact: 1-800-223-7978
> Web: http//www.sisuent.com

Also, *The Jewish Video Catalog* listed above has videos for kids.

Kids' Books

In God's Name, by Sandy Eisenberg Sasso, published by Jewish Lights

> This beautiful little book is a nice way to introduce a child to the idea of God. For that matter, adults could use the book for the same purpose. The story it tells is simple, yet profound.

The Five Books of Moses for Young People, by Esta Cassway, published by Jason Aronson

> If you want to introduce elementary school children to the Jewish master stories of the Bible, this is the book for you. This author has a way of speaking to children. Even though the book refers to God as a He, I think most adults and children would really appreciate this effort to make the Bible understandable and captivating.

Organizations

You may wish to contact one or more of the following, depending on your interests:

Environment:

Coalition on the Environment and Jewish Life: Caring for the environment is what these people are about. They can show you a rich Jewish tradition in environmentalism that will make you proud and help make this a safer, cleaner planet.

> 443 Park Avenue South
> New York, NY 10016
> Phone: 212-684-6950
> Web: http//www.coejl.org

Feeding the Hungry:

Mazon: A Jewish Response to Hunger: These folks set out to capture three percent of what Jews spend on food at parties, bar/bat mitzvahs, Passover seders, and so on, and distribute the money to the hungry. Today they are considered one of the leading hunger-fighting organizations in the world. This is another organization that will make you proud to be Jewish. Reach them at:

> Mazon
> 1990 South Bundy Drive, Suite 260
> Los Angeles, CA 90025-5232
> Phone: 310-442-0020
> Web: http//www.mazon.org

Health:

National Center for Jewish Healing: If you are hurting, know someone who is ill, or are in the medical profession — do yourself a favor and call these people. They can show you that Judaism is an incredibly therapeutic and compassionate tradition.

> National Center for Jewish Healing
> 850 7th Avenue, Suite 1201
> New York, NY 10019
> Phone: 212-399-2320

Jewish Ritual/Hebrew:

National Jewish Outreach Program: Want to learn to read Hebrew in just 7½ hours, or want a crash course in the basics of traditional Judaism or celebrating a traditional Sabbath? These folks offer such courses all over the country — call or write them at:

NJOP
989 6th Avenue, 10th Floor
New York, NY 10018
Phone: 1-800-44HEBREW
Web: http//www.njop.org

Spirituality:

National Havurah Committee: If you want to meet people in your area who are interested in exploring Jewish spirituality in small group settings, this committee is for you. They are a central address for havurahs all over the country. You can contact them at:

National Havurah Committee
7135 Germantown Avenue — Second Floor
Philadelphia, PA 19119-1824
Phone: 215-248-1335
Web: http//www.havurah.org

A History of the Jews

by Paul Johnson

Excerpted from the introduction to A History of the Jews:

Is history merely a series of events whose sum is meaningless? Is there no fundamental moral difference between the history of the human race and the history, say, of ants? Or is there a providential plan of which we are, however humbly, the agents? No people has ever insisted more firmly than the Jews that history has a purpose and humanity a destiny. At a very early stage in their collective existence they believed they had detected a divine scheme for the human race, of which their own society was to be a pilot. They worked out their role in immense detail. They clung to it with heroic persistence in the face of savage suffering. Many of them believe it still. Others transmuted it into Promethean endeavors to raise our condition by purely human means. The Jewish vision became the prototype for many similar grand designs for humanity, the perennial attempt to give human life the dignity of a purpose.

Copyright 1987, HarperCollins Publishers.
Used with permission.

"...We are people of memory and prayer. We are people of words and hope. We have neither established empires nor built castles and palaces. We have only placed words on top of each other. We have fashioned ideas; we have built memorials. We have dreamed towers of yearnings — of Jerusalem rebuilt, of Jerusalem united, of a peace that will be swiftly and speedily established in our days."

Israeli President Ezer Weizman
Speech to the German legislature
January 16, 1996

A Few Parting Comments

I wrote this book because it seems to me that far too often nowadays, Jews and Judaism are two ships passing in the night. This is a shame and need not be the case. Based on what I have learned about Jews and Judaism while working on this book, there is a lot of potential for connection.

I say this because I believe the three main benefits Judaism offers are the same three things most Jews (and all people, for that matter) seem to be looking for in their lives. Specifically, I am referring to ethical guidance, spiritual satisfaction, and a sense of belonging. Now that you have read this book, I hope you can see that there are a lot of meaningful ways to "get more out of being Jewish."

Now What?

As I have stated from the outset, the intent of this book is not to convince you to adopt any level of practice or affiliation. This book is meant to be a "Judaism appetizer" that is intriguing enough for you to want to taste more.

If it has whetted your appetite, please consider one or more of the following user-friendly next steps. Your first reaction to some of them could be "no way." Still, I suggest you look into them anyway—you may be pleasantly surprised.

1. **Sample any of the items** listed in the bibliography at the end of the last chapter.

2. **Ask questions** about Judaism! You can start by simply having a dialogue with friends and relatives. Ask people who are knowledgeable—they do not have to be rabbis.

3. At the same time, don't be afraid to **ask a local rabbi** if he or she would candidly talk to you about their notion of God or why they choose

Judaism for themselves — or pick any subject. Also tell them candidly what you think.

4. Share this book with some friends. Then, **get together and talk** about what you thought of each chapter.

5. **Visit www.BeingJewish.org** based on the ESP circles in this book. At this website, you will find columns, articles, and other resources to help you answer one or all three of these questions: How can I be a more **Ethical** person? How can I have a richer Jewish **Spiritual** life? How can I enhance my sense of belonging to the Jewish **People**? I hope you'll spend some time here!

6. **Check out what classes** about Judaism are available at your local Jewish Community Center (JCC), Jewish Federation, college, synagogue, or temple.

7. **Take a trip to Israel!** You cannot visit Israel without getting in touch with being Jewish — whatever that means for you. (Israel is not necessarily a religious experience.) No two people react the same way to Israel — but most come back enriched by the journey.

8. Before bidding you adieu, I offer you the following next step: **Speak up!** In doing the research for this book, I heard from a lot of people who expressed unhappiness with different aspects of Jewish life. If you feel that way as well, I want to encourage you to express yourself constructively — ideally with suggestions on how to improve things.

   Share your ideas with people in positions of authority: rabbis, principals, teachers, presidents, executive directors, and board members of Jewish institutions and organizations. If nothing else, send your thoughts in writing to me. Jewish leaders need and deserve to know what you are thinking. If you keep your thoughts to yourself, there is little or no chance that your concerns will be fixed. As the popular 1960s civil rights slogan said, "You are either part of the problem or part of the solution."

In Conclusion

To sum up, I offer a one-sentence answer to the question: Why be Jewish? My response: I think Judaism is good for the world because it is about making people be the best they can be. Of course, the U.S. Army makes a similar claim. Judaism could learn a thing or two about marketing from the Army.

For as I mentioned in the introduction to this book, lately Judaism has found that sales are down in spite of the fact that our R&D department over the last 2,000 years, has produced an excellent product. But don't take my word for it; try some of the choices listed above under "Now What?" I am optimistic that you will be pleased with what you will find while pursuing Judaism.

To me, this book will have been a success if in its pages you have found some ways to establish or reestablish a connection with your Judaism. If you are already involved Jewishly, and this book strengthens your feelings and understanding of Judaism, then to me that, too, is success. Finally, if you work with Jews as a lay or professional leader, my dream would be that this book serve as a door opener that you can use to help others find a connection to Judaism.

In closing, I'd like to say thank you. I care deeply about Judaism and I also realize your time is valuable, so I am very appreciative of your taking the time to read my book. My sincere hope is that in these pages you have found many ways to get more out of Judaism. I also hope our paths will cross again. Please see the last two pages of this book for ways that might happen. Thanks again.

Rather than

tear this sheet out,

please photocopy

the reverse side,

or

JUST CALL:
1-800-304-9925
THANK YOU!

Order Form

FAX   Fax orders: Photocopy, fill out and fax this page to 763-542-0171.

☎   Telephone orders: **Call toll free 1-800-304-9925** or 763-545-3666. Have your VISA or MasterCard ready.

▆   On-line orders: LeoPublish@aol.com or www.BeingJewish.org.

✉   Postal orders: Photocopy, fill out and mail this page to Leo & Sons Publishing, 175 Oregon Avenue South, Minneapolis, MN 55426.

Please send the following books:

_____ copies of *How To Get More Out of Being Jewish Even If…*

Copies	Discount*	Unit Price*	Shipping & Handling*
1–2		$14.95	$3.00
3–5	15%	$12.70	$6.00
6–10	20%	$11.95	$9.00

*Prices subject to change.

For more than 10 copies, call 1-800-304-9925 for volume discounts.

Sales tax: Please add 6.5% sales tax for orders shipped to Minnesota addresses.

❏ I would like information about other books and material by Gil Mann.

Date: _____

Total [＿＿＿＿＿]

Please send the books to:

Name _____

Address _____

Address _____

City _____ State _____ ZIP _____-_____

Day Telephone (_____)_____

Payment:

❏ Check – mail order only   ❏ VISA   ❏ MasterCard

Card Number _____

Name on Card _____ Expiration Date _____ / _____

Call toll free and order now: 1-800-304-9925

Gil Mann
c/o Leo & Sons Publishing
175 Oregon Avenue South
Minneapolis, MN 55426

Fax: 763-542-0171
E-Mail: MannGil@aol.com
Website: www.BeingJewish.org

Dear Reader:

As I mentioned in the introduction, the response to this book since it was first published in 1996 has been so positive that a series of developments have occurred. They give me the opportunity to stay in touch with readers and I want to invite you to take advantage of these developments.

The easiest way for us to stay in touch is via the website I created called www.BeingJewish.org. Please check out the website and feel free to send in your emails!

The email I have received since this book was published, has been so compelling that I began selecting one per week and responding publicly in a column that has been syndicated to Jewish papers all over North America and on Jewish websites. The column is called Jewish Email or Email of the Week. If you go to www.BeingJewish.org and click on Email of the Week you can read these columns and also send in your comments.

Additionally, I have started publishing a magazine called *Being Jewish…Relevant Judaism for Modern Life.* On the last page of this book is information about getting a free copy of *Being Jewish* Magazine.

I welcome your visits and even more, your emails about this book or any Jewish issue or experience you care to share.

Finally, I have written a new book featuring the best of the thousands of emails people have sent to me. Based on feedback I have heard, this second book is both enjoyable and helpful to readers. I hope you'll agree. To order the book or learn more, please go to **www.BeingJewish.org** or call **1-800-304-9925.**

I look forward to crossing paths with you again soon!

Gil Mann

If you liked this book, you'll love:
www.BeingJewish.org
&
Being Jewish Magazine... Relevant Judaism for Modern Life!

— Published by
Gil Mann

The website and magazine are as readable as *Reader's Digest,* only more user friendly! You will find them filled with relevant, enjoyable and valuable information and inspiration about the Jewish way of life.

Gil has taken the ESP circles introduced in his book to select and organize the magazine and website. All the content is designed to help you look at your modern life and our ancient tradition and answer one or all three of these questions:

E — How can I be a more Ethical person?

S — How can I have a richer Jewish Spiritual life?

P — How can I enhance my sense of belonging to the
Jewish People?

Every article is carefully selected and edited so that all concepts are easily understood even by those of use who left the synagogue as teenagers and did not return for 20 years or more!

Being Jewish Magazine and www.BeingJewish.org will show you ways to access each of the ESP circles and where they overlap, so that in your modern life, you can more fully enjoy the wisdom and beauty of *Being Jewish!*

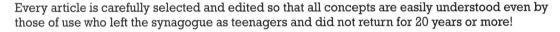

For a free copy of *Being Jewish* Magazine, send a self addressed 9"x12" envelope affixed with 55¢ postage to:

Being Jewish
175 Oregon Avenue South
Minneapolis, MN 55426